The
PRICE
Paid for
CHARLEY

OTHER BOOKS BY EARL B. PILGRIM

Sea Dogs and Skippers (contributor)

Will Anyone Search for Danny?
Curse of the Red Cross Ring
The Ghost of Ellen Dower
The Captain and the Girl
Blood on the Hills

The PRICE Paid for CHARLEY

SECOND EDITION

Earl B. Pilgrim

FLANKER PRESS LTD.
ST. JOHN'S, NL

Library and Archives Canada Cataloguing in Publication

Pilgrim, Earl B. (Earl Baxter), 1939-
  The price paid for Charley / Earl B. Pilgrim. -- 2nd ed.

ISBN-10 1-897317-05-6

  1. Grenfell, Wilfred Thomason, Sir, 1865-1940. 2. Missionaries,
Medical--Newfoundland--Biography. I. Title.

FC2193.3.G7P55 2007   610.69'5092   C2007-901519-0

© 1990, 2007 by Earl's Books

ALL RIGHTS RESERVED. No part of the work covered by the copyright hereon may be reproduced or used in any form or by any means—graphic, electronic or mechanical—without the written permission of the publisher. Any request for photocopying, recording, taping or information storage and retrieval systems of any part of this book shall be directed to Access Copyright, The Canadian Copyright Licensing Agency, 1 Yonge Street, Suite 800, Toronto, ON M5E 1E5. This applies to classroom use as well.

PRINTED IN CANADA

Cover Design: Adam Freake

This paper has been certified to meet the environmental and social standards of the Forest Stewardship Council® (FSC®) and comes from responsibly managed forests, and verified recycled sources.

FLANKER PRESS
PO BOX 2522, STATION C
ST. JOHN'S, NL, CANADA
TOLL FREE: 1-866-739-4420
WWW.FLANKERPRESS.COM

9 8 7 6 5 4

We acknowledge the financial support of the Government of Canada through the Canada Book Fund (CBF) and the Government of Newfoundland and Labrador, Department of Business, Tourism, Culture and Rural Development for our publishing activities. We acknowledge the support of the Canada Council for the Arts, which last year invested $153 million to bring the arts to Canadians throughout the country. *Nous remercions le Conseil des arts du Canada de son soutien. L'an dernier, le Conseil a investi 153 millions de dollars pour mettre de l'art dans la vie des Canadiennes et des Canadiens de tout le pays.*

To Pascoe Simms, who passed away in February 1990. We have lost a great friend, and St. Anthony a true son.

Real joy comes not from ease or riches or from the praise of men, but from doing something worthwhile.

> Sir Wilfred Thomason Grenfell

Preface

I would like to say to the readers of this book, and especially those who have never read or heard about the work of Dr. Sir Wilfred T. Grenfell, that the more I researched the life of this great man, the more fascinated I became. I was privileged to be able to interview many of the people who worked closely with him.

While it is true that he was a humanitarian and had a great love for people, he was also an organizer and a keen businessman. In addition he was a sportsman, an entertainer, and a diplomat. His personality was such that he could make one both laugh and cry at the same time. But most of all he was a medical doctor. There is no doubt that Wilfred T. Grenfell was a genius. All who knew him admitted it, even though he made many costly mistakes, the biggest being the loss of support from the Newfoundland Government. His letters and historical documents show that many of his projects in Newfoundland and Labrador failed due to lack of governmental support and drive.

When Dr. Grenfell arrived in St. John's in 1892, it was still smoldering from the Great Fire that levelled the city. Any chance of securing financial help at that time was out of the question. His hospital ship moved north, flying the flag of the Mission to Deep Sea Fishermen.

Can we imagine his reaction when he stepped ashore in a small town that had never seen a dentist? Dr. Grenfell found lice in abundance. Tuberculosis, beriberi, and scurvy were rampant. Many people were missing limbs. People amputated fingers and toes, and even the legs and arms of their children if it meant saving their lives. The suffering of childbearing was reminiscent of the Stone Age.

The doctor was no product of the English industrial empire controlled by merchants. In Newfoundland at the turn of the twentieth century, merchants were the emperors. In northern Newfoundland and Labrador, Dr. Grenfell saw the horrible depths of poverty and the terrible suffering that came at the hand of the economic model known as the "truck" system. After interviewing the residents he learned that the government never offered a helping hand; everything was left with the fish merchants, who operated through barter. Fishermen obtained supplies once a year in return for their catch. Most of the time they did not break even. Even if they did, they had to take their balance in supplies. Dr. Grenfell noted all of this, and he also saw potential: those living along the coast were great people, but had never been given a fair chance.

For these and many other reasons, Dr. Grenfell decided to do something. He set out to organize the people by setting up co-operatives, which, of course, stepped on the toes of the fish merchants. The doctor was recalled from Newfoundland to England and was replaced, but his faith and determination were such, however, that a few years later he returned to the island and picked up where he had left off. The people of northern Newfoundland, Labrador, and the Quebec North Shore eagerly anticipated his return, often referring to him as a saint.

His scheme included setting up headquarters on the Great Northern Peninsula, and establishing a string of nursing stations both along the coast and from the Quebec North Shore to northern Labrador. He would recruit nurses and doctors from Great Britain and the United States. First he went to St. John's, where he unsuccessfully requested financial help. However, he didn't walk away empty-handed; he was granted permission to acquire land on which he could erect hospitals and nursing stations. He was also given timber rights to Canada Bay, the Great Northern Peninsula's prime stands. This area satisfied his need for construction supplies.

Next Dr. Grenfell looked for a suitable location for his headquarters. He would have to build near the ocean and as close as possible to his timber supply. Calling a public meeting, he announced his plan to erect his headquarters and a large hospital in the general vicinity of Englee. The meeting progressed smoothly until he mentioned that he had secured the timber limits around the bay. The meeting turned chaotic. Those attending decided against allowing him in the area. The doctor then moved farther north to the little fishing village of Conche, on the eastern shore of the Great Northern Peninsula.

Again a public meeting was held. Those in attendance unanimously approved Dr. Grenfell's building his headquarters at Conche.

However, as soon as he left Conche, another meeting, regarding the same matter, was called. Some pointed out that, if the doctor were permitted to proceed with his endeavour, one hundred per cent of Roman Catholics living in Conche could lose their identity. They felt that Dr. Grenfell would bring in hundreds of workers who would disrupt their form of worship. A letter was drafted, informing Dr. Grenfell that he would not be permitted to build his headquarters at Conche. He then proceeded to St. Anthony, where he was received with open arms.

Grenfell's work in St. Anthony attracted people from all over the world, and if one followed him for a few months during his busy years, one would have found him sitting at the banquet tables of some of the wealthiest and most famous people of his time. A few days later, however, he would sit in a lowly abode along the rocky coastline of northern Newfoundland, giving medical attention or helping someone who was hungry. He was not afraid to ask the rich for help nor tend to the poor. It was not uncommon to see Dr. Grenfell entering a home on a stormy night in answer to a call. He would open his medical bag, put his patient on a table, and perform major surgery without hesitation. He was a tremendous worker.

While digging into the story of the life and work of Dr. Grenfell, I discovered many beautiful things about Lady Grenfell, his beloved wife. I learned that she was the great driving force behind the man. She was an organizer, especially so in gathering clothing and household items in the United States. She was also a tremendous help in looking for the latest medical equipment and up-to-date drugs. In addition she sent gifts to needy families on the Great Northern Peninsula.

This story is based on fact. Although the book may not describe exactly what happened nearly a hundred years ago, I hope that it will be the same in its historical context, and that you will be prepared to go back and walk in the footsteps of the great pioneer and builder, Sir Wilfred Thomason Grenfell.

Today many people maintain that Dr. Grenfell was an opportunist, that he came along at the right time, that the world was young and the land ready to be taken. On that note, I believe that now is the time for others to become pioneers, starting with the environment. Maybe a hundred years from now, someone can tell a story about you!

Prologue

THE MORNING OF THURSDAY, January 9, 1908, dawned clear but chilly with a northeasterly wind. The temperature had dropped thirty degrees below zero, but the day still looked promising for Roddickton. The sun cast its rays over a huge uncut forest which was unspoiled but for a nearby sawmill owned by Dr. Grenfell.

After lighting a fire in the Comfort stove, Skipper Jim Hancock used his knife to scrape the half-inch-thick frost from the windowpane and took a peek outside. A glorious scene greeted him. The Cloud Hills loomed in the distance and snowdrifts etched along the bay, looking like the work of a scribe who had written in a foreign language and then retraced the writing with a pale red ink. The steam from Skipper Jim's breath clouded his view, so he regretfully withdrew from the window.

He had been up most of the night with Charley, his youngest son. The boy had recently gotten sicker than usual, so the night before last, Jim and his wife, Fanny, had decided they would move to Englee. This was a small town in a sheltered harbour on the northern headland of Canada Bay. Only one other family, the Reids, resided in Canada Bay this winter. Theirs was a permanent home, ten miles away, where the Hancocks could obtain a backup supply of homemade medicine.

Jim and Fanny Hancock had five sons and three daughters. Of their boys, Roy, Will, Joe, and Mark were able-bodied men, but Charley had been sick most of his life. He was crippled from birth and spent his fifteen years fighting infections, colds, and other illnesses, to which his condition had left him susceptible. Now a new illness had crept up on him and worsened with each passing day.

"Hey, Mark!" Jim called. "Get up! What a day this is going to be!"

Mark made a noise in his room.

Jim raised his voice. "I think while we're out to Englee we'll haul in a barrel of potatoes."

"Good enough," Mark grunted. "I'll get the dogs harnessed."

Mark Hancock swung his legs over his bed and stood on the cold floor. His bed, if you could call it that, was simply a wooden frame nailed to the wall and filled with duck feathers. He was twenty years of age and already a giant of a man, with a barrel chest and treelike limbs all covered with hair. His head looked unnaturally small, perched on top of such a large body. He was a little clumsy but had the endurance of a polar bear, and he was a capable young man besides, able to sit and play with a child or fight like a tiger, whatever the situation demanded. Working in extreme temperatures was no problem for him, whether in a heavy parka in the blazing summer sun or in his shirt sleeves in twenty-below weather.

Hitching up his canvas pants and braces, he walked into the kitchen and blew a jet of steam from his nostrils, like a horse snorting itself awake on a brisk autumn morning.

"Is the kettle boiled, Father?"

"No, but the water is."

Mark grinned. His father, Jim, was full of wit. Although amenities were scarce, morale was high in the Hancock family. The young man sat at the table with a thick slice of molasses-coated bread and an enamel mug filled with steaming tea. He gulped his breakfast and lumbered back to his room, dressed in a long suit of underwear, pulled on his skin-boots, and slipped into his pants and shirt. He re-entered the kitchen just as his older brother, Joe, stirred.

"There's an awful commotion here this morning, gang," Joe said. "What's going on, Father?"

"That's pretty easy to figure out," said Jim. He looked at Mark and winked. "A commotion for sure, Joe, now that you're up."

"Never mind the wisecracks, Father! Did I hear someone say you're going to Englee this morning?" When neither his father nor his brother answered, he frowned. "I say, did I hear someone say they're going to Englee this morning?" He stared at Jim, waiting for an answer.

Mark said, "Father, who's supposed to answer that?"

"Answer what?"

Joe started to laugh. "Okay, okay. So you're going to Englee and you don't want anyone else to go. Right? What are you going out for?"

"A barrel of potatoes."

"Oh," said Joe, astonished. "Potatoes, hey?" He walked to the stove and poured himself a mug of tea. "'Tis a pretty cold morning. Do you know what you should do?" He tasted his tea and reached for a slice of bread. "You should get the coach box and lash it to your komatik." A coach box was a large wooden box used to carry passengers.

"Enough, Joe," his father piped up, "for I'll have you know that I don't need a coach box to keep me warm. Don't you worry about that."

"It's not for you, Father," said Joe. "It's about forty below outside. I figured you'd need the coach box to put the potatoes in to keep them from freezing."

The entire family was up and about when Mark Hancock went outside to prepare the komatik. He and his father decided to wait until they reached Englee to line a box with sawdust to protect the potatoes. Eight hardy dogs were picked from the pen and brought to the komatik, which was tied to a tree stump by a drug, the chain-loop used to rein the dog team.

Skipper Jim Hancock was about to board the komatik when Joe rushed from the house.

"Father," he said, "why don't you get something to sit on, like a box or something? If you sit on the bars with your fingers down through, you could lose a few if you happen to strike a stump or something." Bars were cross-braces, four by one inches thick, used to strengthen a komatik, which is about thirty inches wide.

Skipper Jim considered his son's suggestion. "You're right." He added with a grin, "Someone get me the coach box."

"Listen, Father," Joe continued. "Why don't you get that butter tub from the woodhouse and lash that to the komatik to sit on? It'll be easier on your back, too."

"Good idea."

Mark strapped the empty, eighteen-pound tub firmly to the komatik and proceeded to hook up the dogs. When the first four were in place, they strained to dash ahead. When two more were put in position, the team went wild.

Joe warned, "That's enough, Mark! You'll kill the old man."

"Don't you be silly!" said Mark. He attached the remaining two, and the eight dogs howled to move, biting and snapping at each other. Hopping aboard the komatik, he shouted over the noise, "Get on her, Father! Get on her and hold on! Hold on, I say! Make sure you grab on tight!" He gripped a small wood split in his hand.

Skipper Jim mounted the tub and grasped the rope. Mark pulled the komatik back, then released the drug. The dogs leaped ahead, and for a moment it seemed that Skipper Jim would be staying home! His body appeared to float in mid-air. Suddenly the rope he was holding grew taut and he was jolted forward. He pulled himself upright.

"Father," shouted Mark, "hold onto yourself! My jingles, Father, you almost lost your underwear!"

"Never mind, you. Drive the dogs! Just drive the dogs!"

Mark laughed.

The first couple of miles out of Roddickton were pleasant and uneventful. The five-mile road shot through dense forest and flat country. Halfway across the neck Skipper Jim shouted for Mark to stop. With all the dogs pulling, they were moving too quickly, too recklessly.

Mark struggled to bring the team to a halt, and his father stepped down.

"You listen, Mark!" he said. "Unhook four of these dogs right now."

Mark was sweating as he obediently tied the komatik to a tree and unhooked four dogs. Then he tucked his woollen mitts into his pockets. The dogs barked furiously and steam rose from their mouths. Some scratched their toenails in the snow. Others bit their teammates.

Skipper Jim climbed aboard for the second time. Mark untied the sled and they continued their flight, pulled along by only four dogs, while the others ran free alongside. Mark tapped the sled with the wooden split. He squawked like a crow, urging the dogs on. "Hark! Look at the crow!"

The dog team raced with abandon.

They soon arrived at the spot where the community of Bide Arm now rests. Mark stopped his team and hooked up the other four dogs while Skipper Jim buttoned his canvas coat. They now had open bay all the way to Englee. A few days ago travellers had passed Jim Hancock's log cabin in Roddickton and reported strong ice in the direction they were headed. The

THE PRICE PAID FOR CHARLEY

sea had pushed in and broken up the ice, which now extended more than halfway up the arm. The arm had since frozen over again.

On this frosty morning as Mark and his father concentrated on the dog team and the snowdrifts, they failed to notice the open water spreading before them. Mark tapped the komatik and encouraged the animals to move. They were soon skimming over extremely slippery ice.

"My jingles, Father!" Mark cried above the barking dogs. The lead dog lost its footing and fell. The ice could not bear the dog's weight and it plunged into the water, dragging the others with it.

Mark reacted quickly. He had been around dogs all his life, and he felt that he knew how they behaved in situations like this. Dogs in water will climb onto anything within reach. To avoid tumbling into the open water, he jumped to the left, and his huge body crashed onto the ice, sending a network of cracks all around him. He tried to regain his breath, but then the ice beneath him gave way and he plunged into the frigid water. The cold jarred him and cleared his head. Seconds later panic overtook him when he looked up to find a solid ceiling of ice directly overhead; in the confusion he had drifted several feet away from the hole the weight of his body had made, and now he was trapped. Without thinking he shot a fist upward, punching through the two-inch barrier with ease.

He broke through and glanced toward his father to see the komatik perched above the partly submerged dogs. Skipper Jim had been thrown from the butter tub and had lodged between the noses of the sled. Although he was by no means a champion swimmer, Mark could at least stay afloat. His instincts took over as he was forced to choose between life and death. Stabs of pain shot through him as his head went under. When he resurfaced his massive arms made wide arcs as he struggled to stay afloat. He slashed the water and, as he resurfaced, he saw Jim gripping the komatik tightly. Mark shouted for him to move toward the tub, but his father seemed in a daze.

Mark let out a horrified scream as, suddenly, the dogs started climbing onto his father. One by one the dogs clawed their way onto the ice, using Jim as a stepping stone. As Mark moved toward the sled, he spied two dogs heading his way, and he knew they would attempt the same thing with him. As his favourite dog—the one he had fondly petted with pride only moments earlier—drew within arm's length, he lifted an enormous fist and delivered a crushing blow between its eyes. The dog collapsed. He spotted another dog swimming toward him, and as it neared he grabbed its head in one hand and held it underwater. When he felt the struggling animal go limp, he released it.

The young man looked toward the komatik again and saw that his father was still holding on, though dogs were all around him, trampling him. He was caught in the dogs' traces and couldn't disentangle himself. He slipped beneath the water again and again while struggling in sheer desperation to push the canines away.

The last thing Mark Hancock heard his father say was "Fanny! Fanny!" before the dogs pushed him under one last time. The weight of the animals then toppled the komatik, and they howled as they sank beneath the unforgiving waves and joined Skipper Jim.

The water doesn't feel so cold after all, Mark thought. He looked toward the shoreline. The solid edge he had just crossed was tapered; he knew he might succeed in pulling himself over it. He struck out for the shore.

He felt something around his legs. Something had snagged above his knees and he couldn't move them. He must have hooked a piece of rope or something, he figured, but the thought only renewed his determination to reach his goal. Weighing the odds and openly defying them, he let out a roar and moved toward the shoreline at a heroic pace.

At one point he turned and scanned the area where the komatik had been. *Father has drowned for sure*, he thought dejectedly. "Is it possible that Father is gone?" he whispered.

Suddenly an inner voice commanded, *Fight! Fight! Move! Move!*

He obeyed.

The shoreline drew nearer and Mark's knees struck bottom. He stumbled ashore a few steps and fell on his face into the salty snow. He sucked air into his lungs just before everything faded from his eyes.

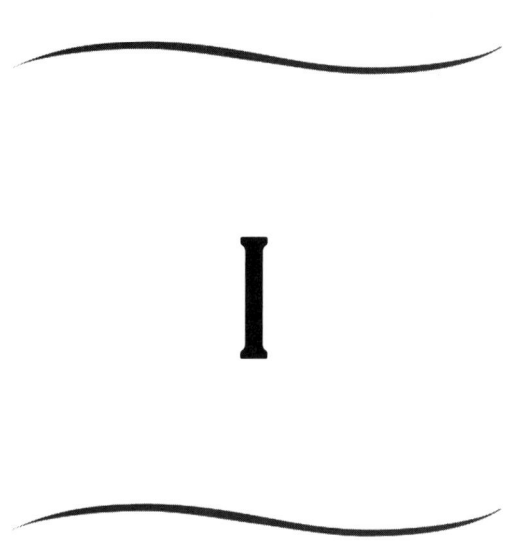

1

JOHN WILCOX OF ENGLEE was a tall, broad-shouldered man with a square jaw. With his heavy moustache he looked more like a statesman than a law enforcement officer. He lived in a large, two-storey house, and most of the furniture in it he had bought himself. Most visitors to Englee dropped by his place. The judge, policeman, and Methodist minister visited occasionally and stayed there. His most frequent visitor was the English doctor, Wilfred Grenfell, who used Wilcox's home as a clinic whenever he visited Englee. John Wilcox's was a busy house that served as a business centre, hospital, and law firm combined.

Wilcox was the local game warden in an era when methods of travel were primitive. He didn't own a dog team, but conducted wildlife patrols on foot, using snowshoes in winter and rowboat in summer. Caribou was the only big game in need of protection; moose had been introduced to the Gander Bay area a few years earlier, but none yet roamed in northern Newfoundland.

On this frosty morning Wilcox didn't need to take to the high country in search of poachers. Instead he set out on a woods road to the bottom of Bide Arm to check his rabbit snares as the rising sun cast its splendid rays over the surrounding foliage. He snowshoed through the snow, observing that some house windows were boarded over. The inhabitants had gone for the winter to Canada Bay, where they cut logs for the Grenfell Mission. Some houses were nearly hidden by snow, with only their stovepipes poking out to mark their existence.

Wilcox continued walking the trail and past the last house, digging out his snares as he went. He reached the bottom of Bide Arm and went over the ridge for a mile or so, where he stopped to light a fire and boil some water. He thought he heard dogs barking, but decided it was just his imagination.

It is unknown how long Mark Hancock lay face down in the snow, with his feet and legs in the icy water of the North Atlantic. Human flesh can stand only so much cold before it freezes, unless the blood is in continuous circulation.

Mark's senses cleared. Rolling over he lifted his head and felt a rush of cold air on his face. He pushed himself up and stared at the backs of his hands. They were bleeding. He tried in vain to move his legs. Something was wrapped around them. On closer inspection he saw that his suspenders had snapped, allowing his pants to fall just below his knees. With great effort he struggled to his feet.

THE PRICE PAID FOR CHARLEY

Mark felt the frost biting into every part of his body. He reached down to haul up his pants, but his hands were numb and did not respond. The strength had ebbed from them. He tried to get moving, but strength had left his legs as well.

"What can I do?" he asked in desperation.

He had no knife to sever his pants. He didn't care whether he wore pants or not at this point; he only wanted his legs free. His clothes were beginning to freeze, and his arms stiffened. He jumped into the water, reached down, and grabbed his pants. The water took some of the numbness out of his hands and softened his frozen pants.

He clamped his teeth and pulled. The pants began to give, and he managed to pull them just above his knees. He could now walk a little. Holding onto his pants with one hand and straightening up, he stepped out of the water. As he did his canvas coat made a cracking noise.

Somewhere in the woods, he thought, *there's a trail.*

Mark staggered toward the trees near the shoreline. He was waist-deep in snow. It clung to him as he shuffled along, the blood dripping from his hands marking twin red trails in the powder on either side of the furrow he plowed.

He had gone approximately a hundred feet when he saw snowshoe tracks heading into the country and toward Roddickton. He knew that Englee was the closest town—only four miles distant—so he turned in that direction. His pants, now ice-encrusted, stayed up on their own. He couldn't move his hands, and his feet and legs were numb, tripping him as he went, but each time he painfully struggled to his feet.

"My good Lord," he cried as he trampled the snowshoe tracks. "I'm freezing all over!"

Brute strength and determination alone pushed him onward.

John Wilcox drank the last of his tea and placed his utensils back into his packsack. He looked around.

"'Tis beginning to blow," he said. "Wind is from the northwest. Got to get back before I freeze to death."

Stepping into his snowshoe tracks, he began his return journey. In places his tracks were already covered. He glanced at his watch. A quarter past one.

To pass the time Wilcox thought about conditions on the coast, and in Newfoundland in general. After hearing from Dr. Grenfell and others of the prosperity in Canada, the United States of America, and Great Britain, he despaired he would ever see the day when Newfoundlanders got ahead of the dole. The game warden moved along with axe in hand, his mind jumping from place to place. He stopped. There were fresh tracks ahead, and blood alongside. He bent to examine them closer, but he couldn't identify the creature that had made these prints. Or was it a human? Whatever it was, it was crawling, dragging, and floundering in the snow. And it had come from the ocean.

Stepping into the tracks, Wilcox followed. When he came to the shoreline, he saw a komatik lodged in the ice. Nearby, the bodies of dogs floated low in the water. Whoever had gotten ashore had made quite a commotion on the beach. The trail of blood led him to the water's edge, where its owner had obviously spent some time, either resting or unconscious.

This person cut himself here, he thought.

Wilcox surmised that only one person had come ashore. He could have been carrying someone else, but he doubted it. Giving the abandoned komatik one last glance, he turned and followed the wounded person. The wind was bitter and even John Wilcox, well-dressed as he was, found it difficult to ward off the cold. He marvelled at the stranger's endurance.

"This can be none other than Mark Hancock," he announced, and looked nervously at the trail of blood flanking the tracks. He picked up the pace, expecting to see the wounded young man at every turn in the trail.

At the turn of the twentieth century, Shop-On Cove, located at the entrance to Englee, had been inhabited by the Compton family. Due to the severity of the west and northwest winds, their property had suffered much storm damage, and so they abandoned their houses and stages and moved into a more sheltered area near the town. They took windows, doors, and lumber from their houses, leaving the remains to stand like wooden ghosts shrouded in weathered garments, their outstretched arms ready to welcome the weary traveller.

Mark travelled between Bide Arm and Englee on a trail where a dog team road had been established along the shoreline. He reached Grassy Cove, within a mile of Shop-On Cove. The drift from the wind knocked into him and he fell forward into the snow. His mind still functioned—at least he knew where he was. His legs were like solid blocks and his arms hung like thick icicles. His ears were frozen and his vision came and went, but he kept repeating, "Not here. Not here. I'm not dying here."

Gathering strength, Mark rolled onto his back and forced himself into a sitting position. His massive chest heaved as he took in large gulps of air and yelled at the top of his voice.

"Help!"

Nobody heard him. He fell into the snow again, but again he managed to bring himself to a sitting position. Twisting over, he stood slowly, regained his balance, and headed toward Englee. He didn't know what pushed him, what gave him the courage to move forward, but somehow he managed. He stumbled into the abandoned house of Uncle George Compton and leaned against the wall inside the windswept porch door. Here was blessed shelter from the wind. He had been in this house many times.

Mark began taking stock of himself and the situation. A quick look confirmed that both hands were frozen and locked. His head was the only thing he could move. He closed his eyes, sat, and propped himself up by the wall. He could move no farther. His heartbeat was getting weaker. The end was near.

"I guess this is where I'll die," he said weakly. "Just half a mile from Englee."

A voice pierced the solitude.

"Mark! Hey, Mark!"

Mark opened his eyes. He saw a man he didn't recognize.

THE PRICE PAID FOR CHARLEY

"It's me. John Wilcox."

Wilcox waited for the Hancock boy to respond. When he didn't, he began pressing him for information. The young man was a veritable chunk of ice, and he knew that Mark was about to die.

"Listen, Mark. Who was with you? Was anyone with you?"

"Yes," Mark groaned in anguish. "Father drowned."

"You stay here, Mark, and I'll get help. Try and keep moving. Don't leave this house, okay?"

Mark didn't answer but the game warden nodded as if to reassure himself the boy had heard.

Wilcox ran the half-mile to Englee, shouting as he went. His shouts turned into a scream when he rounded a corner and nearly toppled over a cliff and into the ocean. Years in the outdoors had honed his reflexes, and he quickly righted himself and pressed on toward town.

He darted into the first house he saw, blurting the news as he grabbed a feather mattress from the room and dumped bedclothes onto the floor.

"Call some men. Quickly!" he ordered the surprised owner of the house.

He took the mattress outside to a sled lodged near a woodpile. He threw in a few sticks of wood and placed the mattress on the sled. By now men were running from everywhere as the story got around. John Wilcox sent a few men ahead with blankets as six more grabbed the sled. The game warden called to one of the men en route to the Hancock boy.

"You! Go down and get Aunt Lizzie Gillard right away."

Aunt Lizzie was the local midwife and nurse. Although she had received no formal training, she delivered all the babies and served as a doctor to the sick in the area. She also worked with Dr. Grenfell at his clinic in Englee every two months. The townsman dashed to the opposite end of the harbour in search of her.

The advance party consisting of three men arrived at Uncle George Compton's house in Shop-On Cove and found Mark lying on the ice- and snow-covered floor. One of them rolled him over just as John Wilcox and his company arrived.

"We're too late, John. He's dead."

They surrounded Mark's frozen form, his arms and legs locked rigid. Wilcox knelt and placed his ear to Mark's chest.

"Boys," he stammered, "his heart is still beating!"

"What?"

"He's alive. Get the blankets!"

The rescuers grabbed a homemade quilt, spread it on the floor, and rolled Mark onto it.

"Let's go, boys. Get him on the sled."

As if in a funeral procession, eight men carried Mark from the house and through the drifting snow to the waiting sled. They gently laid him out and secured him, then started walking alongside, heading back to Englee.

Three hundred yards out the rescue party encountered the cliff that had almost doomed the game warden on his way to town. In summer one can only pass the area when the tide is out. In winter the sea freezes, forming a bridge of snow and ice, making it passable but slippery and deadly as the outside edge

THE PRICE PAID FOR CHARLEY

leans out toward the water. The sea was heaving a little now, and the water was thick. It reminded Wilcox of a churning pot of rolled oats.

The group slowed to a crawl. The game warden cautioned, "Boys, we have no time to lose, but we have to be careful."

Halfway along the edge of the cliff, one of Mark's rescuers slipped. Another, positioned on the other side of the sled, also lost his footing. The sled began to slide toward the water. The man on the inside released his grip in order to clutch something and save himself from going over the cliff, and the sled headed straight for the open water. It stopped and dug into a ridge of ice. For several agonizing seconds it rocked there in the wind, but, too late, its momentum caused it to roll onto its side.

There was a sudden jolt, and Mark was tossed into the roiling sea. The water near the shore was six feet deep, but a few feet farther out the shoreline fell away like a shelf. John Wilcox scrambled to the edge of the ice and grabbed another man before he could slide into the water.

"Form a chain!" he shouted. "Form a chain!"

The men held each other's hands in a human chain and pulled up their companion, who had been in serious danger of sinking alongside Mark.

"Look," someone said, pointing to an object in the water. "Grab that! Grab that!"

Reaching down, another man caught a corner of what turned out to be the blanket that encircled Mark. The chain held tightly, and they pulled. Wilcox's heart sank as the blanket unrolled from Mark's stiff body.

"Let me into the water farther, boys," the man holding the blanket said.

He reached down blindly, hoping, until he felt something.

"I've got something! Pull me back!"

"Hang onto it!" said Wilcox, and the men pulled as they backed away from the water's edge.

Like a monster from the deep, Mark Hancock resurfaced, covered in seaweed and slob ice.

2

JOHN WILCOX HEARD SOMETHING that sounded like *My jingles.*

How could this be? This ice grampus was alive? Impossible!

The men carried Mark Hancock across the frozen shoreline and put him back on the feather mattress in the sled. They moved toward town and were soon met by other townsmen and boys who were eager to grab a line and pull. Many questions shot back and forth over Mark's prone form, but no answers were given. They arrived at Aunt Lizzie's house amid a crowd of curious onlookers and stopped the sled. A group immediately picked up Mark and carried him inside. They laid him on a couch that had been moved to the middle of the kitchen.

Several men pronounced Mark dead after giving his frozen body one frightened glance. One woman squeaked in surprise and said, "No, no! He's not dead!" The others looked on and saw what she had seen—the boy's chest was heaving slightly.

"Where's Aunt Lizzie?" Wilcox demanded. "Is she here yet?"

"She's coming now," someone said, and pointed.

Aunt Lizzie burst through the crowd, her knuckles white as she gripped her medicine bag.

"John," she ordered, "get this crowd out."

Most of the onlookers dispersed right away, while others needed a stern reprimand from the game warden before they would move. Two women, relatives of Mark who lived a few houses away, wept helplessly as they watched, offering any assistance they could give. The log cabin at Englee was only a temporary structure, but at least Mark was back in his own neighbourhood, a place where everyone loved and admired him. Aunt Lizzie reached into her bag and extracted a small bottle of brandy. She spooned a drop into Mark's mouth and immediately saw his tongue curl.

She snapped at the two women. "Now, stop your bawling!"

One of the women dried her eyes with her apron.

"Now," she continued, "let's get these clothes off him. Get my scissors in the bag for me. Quickly!"

By now the ice on Mark's clothes was melting in the warm glow of the wood-fed stove. The midwife cut the canvas duck parka down the front and up the sleeves.

"John, here, roll him over for me." Mark's parka was pulled away from him and the heat struck him fully. He groaned.

"I think he's coming to!" one of the women exclaimed.

Aunt Lizzie nodded. "I think so, too. But before he stands on his own two feet again, he'll groan more than that."

She cut Mark's shirt down the back and pulled the ice-caked garment open.

"Roll him onto his back again, John."

Aunt Lizzie expertly cut the sleeves open and pulled off the shirt.

"Now, let's get these boots off."

Mark's sealskin boots were coated with a layer of ice and so stiff that only a heavy kitchen knife would slice through them. Once he was bare-legged, they saw that his feet were frozen.

"He's finished, Aunt Lizzie!" said one of the assistants, and both of them started a fresh round of crying.

Aunt Lizzie glared at them. "Shut up, now!" she said roughly. "None of that foolishness out of you two. Mark Hancock can overcome almost anything."

John saw the doubt in Aunt Lizzie's eyes, but he kept his peace for the women's sake.

"The pants next, John."

Mark's pants were entangled around his knees once again and frozen in place. His thighs were white, frozen chunks. She tore away the lower pants leg.

"Give me the hammer."

Aunt Lizzie gave the stiff pants several knocks with the tool John obediently handed her and finally managed to remove them. All that was left was Mark's knitted woollen one-piece underwear. He groaned and stared at the ceiling. Aunt Lizzie lowered her face to within inches of his. "Mark, can you speak?" Her voice was slow and clear.

The young man let out another pained groan and rolled his head slightly.

"John," Aunt Lizzie said, "he's going to be all right. We'll take care of him now. You get a crowd and go up to the arm to do what has to be done. When you break the news to his family, tell them that Mark will be okay."

Wilcox nodded and left.

"Now, Mark," she said, close to his ear, "you can groan or scream as hard as you like, but I'm going to thaw you out. Do you hear me?"

Steam began to pour out of Mark's ears. In light of the amount of frost covering them, Aunt Lizzie was surprised they had not cracked. "I don't mind your ears," she said. They felt soft and pliable in her hands. "You can live without them. 'Tis your hands and feet that I'm worried about."

Mark screamed in pain. His chest heaved, and he lifted an arm.

"Call one of the men," Aunt Lizzie said to her assistants, who by now had calmed down and dried their tears.

"Yes, ma'am," one said eagerly and hurried out the door.

Jacob Fillier arrived within minutes. He stared at the midwife, then dropped his gaze to the body lying on the couch. "Aunt Lizzie," he offered, "what can I do?"

"Jake, go down and bring me two buckets of salt water right out of the ocean."

"Right away."

She examined Mark's hands. His right pinky finger was swollen and appeared to be broken, there was a cut on his left

THE PRICE PAID FOR CHARLEY

wrist, and a considerable amount of skin had torn from both knuckles; blood seeped from the wounds. "That's good," she said, and sighed in relief. "The blood is beginning to circulate." Mark's elbow was cut badly, too, and though it would require stitches, Aunt Lizzie was satisfied to bandage it for now. His hands and feet were her main concern.

Jacob entered the kitchen carrying two buckets of salt water. "Here they are, Aunt Lizzie," he said, laying them down. He looked at the midwife and then at the water with a curious expression on his face. Mark had just been taken from the salt water, after all. He shrugged and turned to leave.

"You stay here and give us a hand, Jake," Aunt Lizzie said without looking up.

"Okay."

"Help put his hands in the water."

Jacob did as he was told without question. He removed small pieces of ice from Mark's hands and dipped one of the boy's hands into the bucket while Aunt Lizzie looked on. Mark let out another scream as his arm was forced deep into the water, up to his elbow.

One of the assistants went white. She dashed for the door, frightened.

"Keep his arm down!" commanded Aunt Lizzie. "Don't let it come up!"

Jacob kept a firm grip on Mark's arm for a couple of minutes.

"Now, the other one."

Jacob did as he was told. The patient screamed again and tried to grab him with his free hand. Jacob gently released

Mark's hand and moved away. "Aunt Lizzie," he complained, "get another man in here to help us hold him."

People were staring in through the windows. Aunt Lizzie pointed to a young man, Levi Canning, one of Englee's upstanding citizens. Without a word, he ran in.

Looking her patient in the eyes, Aunt Lizzie inquired, "Mark, do you know me?"

He spoke for the first time. "You're Aunt Lizzie."

"You're right!" she said, delighted. "Now, Mark, you listen to me. If you don't do what we tell you to, you could lose both your arms and legs. Just grit your teeth and bear it." She steeled herself as she turned to Jacob and Levi. "All right, boys, put his hands in the bucket."

Levi held one arm down while Jacob dipped the other. Mark screamed but did not struggle. They repeated this four more times.

"Okay, boys. His feet."

Jacob and Levi dragged Mark to the end of the couch. His feet and legs were beginning to thaw as the warmth of the fire spread through the kitchen. They placed the water buckets on the floor, then bent Mark's knees with care, submerging his feet in the brine.

Mark stiffened to a near-sitting position and found his voice again.

"My jingles, Aunt Lizzie! My jingles!"

He fell back on the couch, growling like a caged animal. Sweat streamed from his forehead, his eyes bulged, and his chest was heaving. The growl turned to a high-pitched shriek

THE PRICE PAID FOR CHARLEY

as the pain of recovery began. Aunt Lizzie instructed Levi and Jacob to keep Mark in the water, and she stepped outside.

The roaring fire inside the cabin had melted the frost on the windows, and those outside had a clearer view of the operation. One man later attested that the sounds coming from Mark Hancock were like an old whale that had part of its blowhole stopped up. Levi and Jacob lifted Mark's legs out of the water, and scales of ice fell to the floor. They dutifully immersed his feet again as Aunt Lizzie came in with a plateful of snow and scooped it into the buckets. The midwife then placed a wet cloth on his thighs. Mark grabbed at his hair and ground his teeth as pain racked his body.

"Aunt Lizzie," said a white-faced Levi, "I never saw this done before."

"No more did I," she replied, "but we'll just hope and pray that it'll work. Do you have any other suggestions?"

Levi couldn't offer any.

"Take his feet out, boys."

Mark was breathing rapidly now, and the three realized he was crying.

"Oh my, Aunt Lizzie! Father is drowned! Father is gone! What will we do? Poor Charley, poor Charley . . ."

"Now, Mark," Jacob soothed, "what's done is done. You're lucky."

"I should have drowned instead of Father. The dogs crawled up on him and drowned him. It should have been me!"

"All right, Mark, enough!" Aunt Lizzie barked. "Don't

move." She reached for his foot. "Tell me if you feel anything." She pricked him with a needle.

Mark jumped.

"What foot was that?"

"Left."

Aunt Lizzie nodded and pricked the other foot. Mark groaned in reaction. Satisfied, Aunt Lizzie gave him something for the pain.

"How will I ever be able to counteract the blisters?" she wondered aloud, wringing her hands.

They turned Mark and removed his underwear. The one remaining female assistant tending the fire reddened in embarrassment. She opened the door and stepped out.

Jacob cleared his throat uncomfortably and looked up at the midwife with wide eyes.

Aunt Lizzie grinned. "Don't look at me like that, Jake. I delivered him, and I delivered you, too." Glancing at Levi, she added, "And I delivered you, Levi. As for Mark, I've seen his dirty backside before."

For a moment there was an awkward silence. Levi grinned, and the three of them broke into laughter.

3

HAULING A TRAP PUNT by komatik on the trail from Englee to the bottom of Bide Arm is difficult work in severe cold. Clothing retained little heat, so survival depended mainly on one's internal resistance to the weather. Poor blood circulation in the legs was a common trait of these Newfoundlanders, and arthritis has deformed the hands of many an old-timer on the Great Northern Peninsula, both male and female. Not a few of those hands are missing fingers; if asked why, the old-timers would tell you, "So many chills. So many chills."

On this blustery January evening, a score of men surveyed the ice at the bottom of Bide Arm. The sun hovered low on the horizon and made their shadows reach for the trees. Skipper Jim's komatik lay offshore and would have been unreachable but for the ice the onlookers surmised might be thick enough to walk on. John Wilcox ordered them to follow Jim and Mark's dog team's tracks to the edge of the ice.

"Don't anyone go on the ice until we talk things over," he advised. "Now, boys, listen. It'll be dark soon, so we have to move as quickly as possible. I think the ice is frozen enough to bear a man's weight, so here's what we'll do. Mark said his father's body is tangled in the traces out there, so when we go out we'll have to be careful not to shake him loose.

"We're not interested in the dogs or the komatik. Only Uncle Jim. When we go out we'll have to grab onto him and hang on. There are thirty fathoms of water below him, so if we lose him, we'll be jigging for a week. Let's get some rope and tie it around me and whoever else is going."

A young man named Ambrose Canning volunteered to accompany the game warden to the water's frozen edge. Wilcox tested the ice with an axe and found it thick enough to hold his weight. As he neared the upturned komatik, he spied Uncle Jim's body. Three dogs, kept afloat by the komatik's runners, lay nearby. He motioned to the others to follow. Some were carrying boat oars, and he took one and laid it across the komatik for him to kneel on.

The game warden broke a hole through the glassy ice and touched the dead man's shoulder. To his surprise it was not frozen. He nudged the body a little to the left before brandishing his axe, aiming the flat head toward the edge of the hole he had made. He waved Ambrose back. Soon a heavy silence hung in the air, broken only by his axe's steady chiselling and the occasional eerie moan of the wind.

Fifteen minutes later Wilcox backed away from the gaping hole, satisfied that it was wide enough to proceed. "Get me some rope," he said.

While Ambrose conferred with the men onshore, the game warden blew on his hands to warm them. He gave the ice a

THE PRICE PAID FOR CHARLEY

wary glance and worried that it might have been compromised by the modifications he had made. *It might not be solid enough to hold us now,* he thought nervously. As if in answer, the ice creaked beneath his feet.

Ambrose edged back out to the game warden carrying a thick line. "Here you go," he said.

Wilcox looped an end of the rope around Skipper Jim's arm. He gritted his teeth in concentration and sweat poured down his cheek. He had to move fast; slob ice was already beginning to form in the hole. He placed an oar across the opening and tied the rope to its middle.

"Now, son," he said to Ambrose, "you hoist the oar and lift the body."

On a count of three, Jim Hancock's body was brought out of the water about a foot until his head and shoulders barely crested the lip of the ice. Wilcox quickly looped the rope around the dead man's chest.

"Okay, lift him again."

This time the ice let out a crack as loud as a rifle's report as Ambrose strained against Jim's massive weight.

"Hold it there!" the game warden shouted. He picked up another oar and wedged it between Skipper Jim's legs, propping him up and preventing him from sliding back into the water. Then he removed his frozen wool mitts and took out his pocket knife. He sliced the dogs' traces free from the body with considerable ease. His hands felt numb from just a few seconds' exposure to the cold, and he pulled his mitts back on with some difficulty.

"Now, Ambrose, when I lift the oar under Skipper Jim, put the rope around his waist." The ice groaned around them. "Do you hear that? We've got to hurry! Keep your weight on the other oar, and whatever you do, make sure you tie a good knot in the rope."

"Yes, sir."

Wilcox lifted the body slowly and his companion scrambled to loop the rope around the body's waist..

"Good work, son." He pointed to the shore. "Now, go out there about twenty feet and cut a heel hole in the ice for yourself. Keep this rope fastened around your waist."

Ambrose nodded and took up his new position between the shore and the game warden.

The game warden called to the men onshore. "Take the punt off, boys, and push the komatik out."

They unloaded the boat and on a signal from Wilcox moved the komatik toward him, paying out from the stout rope Ambrose had tied to his waist. Wilcox placed the sled parallel to Skipper Jim and rested his head and shoulders on it. He signalled the men again, and they pulled while Ambrose threw his whole body into tugging the komatik and the dead man from the icy waters.

John Wilcox moved for the shore, and not a moment too soon. Just as he left the komatik's side, the ice toward the rear gave way, and the men hauling on the rope pitched toward the water. At the last possible second, just as the nose of the komatik tipped upward and the vehicle began its slow descent into the water, Ambrose and the others dug in and heaved toward the shore. Wilcox leaped for the rope, lending his strength to the team, and slowly the sled rose above the frosty ledge and arced downward to rest firmly on solid ice. Before long they wrested Jim Hancock from the water entirely. They hauled him close to shore and turned him over. Wilcox and the others worked in silence. They shivered as they laid the body out and placed it in the punt.

"Okay, boys," the game warden instructed. "Get ready to take him back to Englee. When you get there, take him to Uncle Robert Gillard's. He'll make all the funeral arrangements. I'll go on to Roddickton and break the news to his family. I want two men with me and one to go tell my wife that I won't be home tonight."

The two parties left Bide Arm and went their separate ways, one with the body, the other with bad news.

Allan Hancock took charge of the party transporting Jim Hancock's body to Englee. No sooner had they left the ice than a blizzard set in and the betraying sun dropped out of sight. He called his men around him.

"Listen, boys. It's not worth risking our lives taking this body all the way tonight. Let's cover Skipper Jim's body and leave it here in the cove for now."

Having no other choice but to leave the the dead man alone in a blizzard, they wrapped him in sailcloth and laid him in a snowdrift. Marauding animals were an immediate concern, so they laid the trap punt over the body for protection. The wind howled menacingly through the trees as Allan and his group struck for Englee, close together and in single file.

John Wilcox's party encountered the same weather conditions. He and his men continued on the trail with the wind in their faces. There was no turning back; they had to reach Roddickton. A few miles out they met three of the Hancock boys—Joe, Roy, and Will. They had been out looking for their father and brother. Skipper Jim and Mark should have been home before dark, they felt, and they were convinced that something was dreadfully wrong.

It was a sad meeting. The game warden broke the news of their father's demise and their brother's grievous injuries. The Hancocks were a close-knit family. They were a tough breed, but this evening the three brothers wept there on the trail. Their father had always been a solid foundation, always joking with them and keeping morale high on the home front.

Joe calmed a little. "Listen," he said, "we'll survive, but what about poor Charley? What will he do now that Father's gone? I don't think he'll live long, what with his trouble and now this heartbreak. He won't be able to bear up."

John Wilcox and his men allowed the boys this quiet time to mourn. Nobody spoke as the wind whistled and the swirling snow pecked at their faces.

"We'd better move on toward home, boys," the game warden said after a few moments.

"It won't seem like home," Roy moaned. "I wonder what Mother will do when we tell her? I'd say she'll go crazy." He shook his head as if to clear his thoughts. Setting his jaw, he said, "We will just have to face it."

The six men beat their way along the trail to Roddickton,

THE PRICE PAID FOR CHARLEY

covered in snow and ice and carrying a heavy load of sorrow. At midnight they arrived at the log cabin the Hancocks called home. Through the window they could see Charley sitting at the table in a kitchen illuminated by a kerosene oil lamp. His mother was sitting near the stove, staring off into space as she rocked back and forth in the warm glow.

Looking at the woman—their mother—the brothers knew she had not yet heard that she was a widow. They loved their mother. She had spent her more than fifty years working hard to raise a large family. Fanny had raised them well in their home, but now they would repay her by breaking her heart. They were fixed to the spot, wishing that time would stand still and that this moment would last forever.

Wilcox cleared his throat. "Get yourselves together, boys," he murmured.

"All right," said Joe, and without another word he stepped forward and lifted the latch on the door.

"Who's there?" came his mother's nervous voice from inside.

"It's me. Joe."

Fanny Hancock opened the door, and the kerosene glow streamed out from behind her. She searched her son's furrowed brow and trembling mouth.

"Oh my, Joe," she whispered. "You've got bad news." Fanny spoke with a slight English accent, a legacy from her grandfather, Charley Hopkins, one of the first Englishmen to set foot in Englee.

Putting her hands to her face, she turned away and walked

to the table. Joe stepped into the kitchen, and the others followed in silence.

Fanny turned to face the men. Her eyes widened when she saw the game warden, John Wilcox, and she looked for something hopeful in his face. He dropped his gaze to the floor and shuffled his feet uncomfortably. Fanny scanned the faces of the men before her, seeing the same thing in each one.

"Aunt Fanny," Wilcox said, "we've got bad news for you. You're going to have to be strong." He faltered, not knowing what to say next. "Jim fell through the ice," he blurted, "and he is gone."

Fanny's face went white. She staggered to the table and put both hands on it in to steady herself. She turned to regard her youngest son, Charley, as he limped over to them. His eyes were wide and his lip was quivering.

"Is my father gone?" he pleaded. "Will he be coming back?"

Roy let out an anguished cry and leaped to his younger brother's side, catching him in his arms. Charley stared over his shoulder at the men standing in their kitchen. His slender limbs spasmed like a frightened rabbit in a snare with nowhere to go.

4

ALLAN AND HIS GROUP made it to Englee without incident. When he arrived, he stopped to tell Mark what he had done with Skipper Jim's body. "When the storm eases off," he said, "we'll go back to Bide Arm and get your father."

Aunt Lizzie, after examining Mark from head to toe, informed everyone present that he was in perfect shape. Not one blister had appeared on his face. "He might lose his toenails," she had said with a straight face, then grinned. She gave him two large spoonfuls of a black liquid while Allan looked on. Mark's eyes bulged as he swallowed the vile concoction, and he gasped for breath.

"My jingles, Aunt Lizzie!"

He fretted over his father's body lying alone in the snowbank, covered with a trap punt and left behind in forty-below weather, but he nodded weakly and thanked Allan for his efforts. Aunt Lizzie encouraged everyone to leave for home and to be careful in the storm. She asked Allan to drop by her house and tell her husband Robert that she would be sleeping with Mark Hancock. Despite the sorrow, her comment brought laughs from those around her.

An eternity passed at the Hancock house in Roddickton. Everyone was crying, struggling to deal with a new reality. They were trying without much success to come to grips with the news that Skipper Jim Hancock was not coming back.

John Wilcox was growing impatient. Exasperated, the game warden stamped his foot to get the attention of all those in attendance. The Hancocks' lamp rattled on the shelf and almost fell to the floor.

"Listen here," he bellowed, "and shut up. You've got to face it. You could've lost Mark, so you should consider yourselves lucky. Please, you need to comfort each other now."

Fanny brought herself under control. She moved to Charley and laid a comforting hand on his shoulder. "Charley, we're still here," she said, "and we'll love you more than ever."

The crippled boy sobbed helplessly. He rested his head on his arms as the others stood around the table and let their own tears streak their weathered faces.

"I'll get you something to eat, Charley," his mother said, and she turned and walked to the pantry before the boy could reply.

The game warden nudged Will Hancock. "How do you feel?" he asked.

Will sighed. "I've known now for five hours that Father is

gone. I guess I'm getting used to it, and hopefully time will heal the wound."

Early the next day another blizzard hit the area. The men who stayed to help Fanny and her sons managed to reach the shed near the cabin to secure firewood, and a nearby brook for water. Fanny went about her daily chores in silence as she contemplated life without her husband. Not much was said all morning. At the lunch table, however, the topic of burial arose.

"You know your father loved it here." Fanny addressed her sons as they ate. "He often spoke of living here permanently. Do you know what I think he would like? Let's bury him in here, down by the shoreline somewhere."

"Don't be crazy, Mother," Joe said. "We've got a graveyard back home in Englee where all our relatives are buried."

The house was crammed with people, with standing room only. Incredibly, Mark Hancock sat at the table, sipping on his own cup of tea. The only signs of injury on him were the bandages wrapped around his hands. After his ordeal, he was the object of total amazement. *Why aren't his fingers falling off? Why aren't his arms covered in blisters?* Whenever he ate a piece of bread, everybody swallowed with him. He picked up his cup and took a sip, and everyone responded in kind. His friends and family were simply awestruck that the young man had demanded to be transported to Roddickton overnight. Mark had told his story a couple of times, but each time he stopped partway through and broke down and wept. The dogs, his dogs, had trampled his father underfoot and rendered him helpless. He couldn't escape that horrific scene.

Will looked around the room at the gathered townspeople. He was both amazed and touched at the compassion displayed by his fellow man in times of tragedy. He raised his mug of tea and took a few sips before setting it down. "You're right, Mother," he said. "I think Father should be buried here, and I know a good spot right over across the brook. There's a spring there, and the soil is deep. I'm for burying Father there."

A murmur of agreement went around the room.

"Very well, then," said Fanny. "Let's notify everyone."

At two o'clock that afternoon, the storm broke. The wind died and the sun appeared. A soft blanket of snow lay low, shaped by the northeast wind into a lumpy, flowerlike arrangement covering the land as far as the eye could see.

John Wilcox, the game warden, led Joe, Roy, and Will Hancock, and four other men in the knee-deep snow. As they wound their way toward Englee, each took his turn taking the lead to hurry their progress. In places their snowshoes sank so deep the snow fell in around the lead man's steps and had to be trampled. It was slow going and they reached the bottom of Bide Arm by noon. Once they reached the ice, they travelled swiftly over the hard, wind-packed snowdrifts.

A dog team approached, and Wilcox recognized the driver. It was Jacob Fillier, the young man who had helped him and Aunt Lizzie administer aid to Mark Hancock. He slowed and veered toward the group.

"Good day, men. I was just coming in to Roddickton to see you. We had an awful blizzard out home. There are drifts back there ten feet high in some places."

The game warden nodded. "Is there anyone with you?"

"No," said Jacob, "but the crowd just left the cove." He pointed. "They had to leave the body there. They couldn't take it any farther because of the storm. Joe," he continued, "I'm sorry about the death of your father. I know it must be a blow to everybody."

Joe nodded and thanked Jacob for his concern.

"Do you want me to go to Roddickton and get the rest of your family?"

"No, Jake. We're going to bring Father into Roddickton and bury him there."

Jacob wondered why the family planned to bury Skipper Jim in the woods, but he asked no questions. He knew, however, that the minister would have complaints.

John Wilcox interrupted his thoughts. "We're going on to Englee."

"Good enough," said Jacob. "A couple of you can jump on with me if you want."

"Roy," said Wilcox. "A couple of you jump on with Jake, and go on ahead and tell the minister that we're going to bury your father in Roddickton. Don't take any objections. Just tell him we've got our reasons."

Jacob turned the dog team around and set off for Englee with Roy and Will aboard. The game warden and the others headed to the cove, where the body was hidden under the punt.

"I think we'll name this place Deadman's Cove," Joe said.
"Yes, I think we should," Wilcox agreed.
It carries the name to this day.

It took the rest of the day in Englee to prepare Jim Hancock's body for burial. The body was brought to the shed and thawed, the clothing removed and replaced with a Sunday suit. A coffin was constructed and covered with cloth both inside and out. Ten dog teams were harnessed to transport people to and from the funeral scheduled for Sunday afternoon. At noon Saturday the dog team carrying Skipper Jim's body arrived in Roddickton. Not a cloud dotted the sky. Although the sun shone brightly, it produced no heat on this January day. The supreme ruler in the open was Jack Frost, a dictator who stung all within reach.

Fanny had for the most part been able to keep herself under control for the past two days. Charley, however, cried all the time and refused to eat. At night he jittered and wailed, his frail body sweating profusely. At times it was difficult waking him in the morning. Worst of all the family couldn't buy medicine to sedate the mourning teenager. He would have to bear the sorrow of his father's unexpected death alone. Mark recovered enough to resume the tough job of a woodsman. That he was alive was a miracle in itself, not to mention that he had survived the experience with nary a scratch. Life would go on, he assured himself.

The dog team pulled up to the log cabin and the Hancock family peered at them through the window. Eli Fillier walked in. "Aunt Fanny, how are you?" he asked as he placed his arm around her. He was courting her daughter, Elizabeth Jane, and was like a son to her.

Fanny's eyes filled with grateful tears. "I guess I'm as good as can be expected," she said, pushing him gently toward her daughter. Elizabeth Jane was a very pretty young woman, tall and slender with dark-brown hair. She stood alone and hugged herself in her grief, tears streaming down her face. Eli went to her and took her in his arms.

Fanny went to the door and asked the men outside to bring the body to the woodhouse until they were ready. "Eli," she said, "will you be staying for the funeral?"

He nodded.

"Good. It'll be nice to have you here."

Skipper Jim's sons carried the casket to the woodhouse, while the others carried blankets and packages of food into the cabin. Some had even brought feather mattresses, knowing that they would be sleeping on the floor.

Uncle Shem Hancock and his eleven-year-old son, Stanley, were present. "Aunt Fanny," Shem said, "the minister will be here sometime this afternoon."

"That's very nice," she said.

"Has anybody dug the grave yet?"

"Yes, the boys did it," she responded, looking out the window at her sons as they busily stowed their father's body for the coming ceremony.

Uncle Shem went outside and inspected the grave. Skipper Jim's sons had had to dig through four feet of snow just to get to the ground. Before getting to the soil underneath, the diggers also had to contend with a water spring that ran through the earth. Shem surveyed the surrounding dense forest, then looked at the grave, admiring the contrast of white snow and black mud and water thrown up over it. It reminded him of a photograph he'd seen of an inactive volcano. Standing on the snowbank, the bottom of the grave looked far away to Uncle Shem, as a canyon might look to a child.

5

IN THE EVENING THE Methodist minister in the White Bay North Mission, Reverend C. B. Tiller, arrived. A medium-built man, he was rough and ready and was unusually loud in his prayers. He believed one could pray down anything, hallelujah! Life to him meant work, and one might as well get started. Within a few moments of his arrival, the funeral arrangements had been made: six men to carry the casket; a mourners' list prepared; and a breastplate made. The women bent to work, taking over the cooking and cleaning. Sled dogs were everywhere, their owners keeping busy controlling, separating, and feeding the animals.

Charley had always been a sick young man, but today he looked worse than ever. His father had been gone since Thursday, and now, two days later, the young boy's skin had taken on an unhealthy cast and there were dark pockets under his eyes. The fevered bustle and activity around him did nothing to distract him. His mother worried that the grieving period would take a heavier toll on him; she had thought about it in the past few days and decided that, if he did not improve after the funeral, the family would move back to their Englee home. She knew he would feel better there. There were more people to associate with, and other things to preoccupy his thoughts. Also they would be near Aunt Lizzie the midwife, and Emmie Fillier, her replacement. Medical attention would be easier to obtain.

That night a two-hour service was conducted in Fanny's home before everyone retired. Fanny didn't sleep much through the night. She stayed up with Charley, who had developed a lot of pain in his leg. His thigh was swollen and at first she thought it was rheumatism or something less serious, but now it looked like she might be wrong.

The girls gave their room to Reverend Tiller and slept with their mother. It was not his custom to accept the kind offer of somebody's room, but tonight he had to study for his funeral message. After everyone had gone to bed, the only sounds in the night were the crackling of the fire and the soft whisper of Bible pages as the holy man prepared to lay Skipper Jim to rest.

At six o'clock in the morning, the dogs started howling. The light from the stars overhead still bounced off the Cloud Hills and glittered on the ice and snowdrifts on the bay. By seven everybody was out of bed. The three small rooms adjacent to Fanny's and the one used by Reverend Tiller had accommodated the twenty or so guests overnight, and even more were expected by noon today.

Throughout the morning people milled about the kitchen

THE PRICE PAID FOR CHARLEY

and talked in hushed tones about local news and the afternoon funeral. Aside from attending the solemn proceedings and comforting the Hancock family, the social setting lent itself readily to the discussion of near and far events affecting the lives of those living in Roddickton. The townspeople of nearby Englee stayed on and talked of politics and social issues. The reindeer herd owned by the St. Anthony doctor, Wilfred Grenfell, was a big topic of discussion. As usual, the efforts of Dr. Wilfred Grenfell were discussed at length. He was the area's first doctor, who had come clear across the Atlantic from England in 1892 to investigate living conditions on and around the Newfoundland and Labrador coasts. His name held mythic proportions to most of the people in rural Newfoundland, and those who knew him found little to disprove it.

It was thought at first that Charley would not attend the funeral. The family voted against leaving him in the house, however, and wrapped him in blankets for the trip to his father's grave. Soon, Skipper Jim's body was brought into the cabin, and the funeral commenced. After a short prayer everyone joined in singing the words of Isaac Watts's immortal hymn, *O God, Our Help In Ages Past*. There was no musical accompaniment, but this in no way hindered the volume of singing.

After the hymn Reverend Tiller preached a strong, loud, and forceful message for a full half-hour. His voice boomed out over the gathering and echoed throughout the surrounding forest. Skipper Jim Hancock's eulogy was a fitting one, highlighting his life as an important addition to the Newfoundland way of life, one that Newfoundlanders everywhere were made sadder by being snuffed out. The three Hancock girls—Dellah, Telsey, and Elizabeth Jane—wept openly, and their brothers held them all the way through the sermon. Fanny was touched by her children's love for each other, and she collapsed in tears, burying her face in Charley's shoulder.

At his father's graveside Charley sat on a komatik with a blanket pulled around his trembling body. His lips were purple—he was the picture of death, some would say when he was out of earshot. Hot tears coursed down his ashen face. Surrounded by the forest, lost in the snow, Charley sat still and stared with glassy eyes at the hole in the ground where his father lay.

Reverend Tiller put his arm around the young man.

"I'll pray for you, Charley," he said.

The crippled young man remained silent as several men pulled his sled from the grave and toward the cabin. When Charley left, Reverend Tiller nodded to the men at his side. They wordlessly picked up their shovels and covered the remains of fifty-six-year-old James Hancock.

A few days after the funeral, Fanny noticed that Charley's health was diminishing. She realized that the family could no longer remain at the lower end of Canada Bay, that they would have to move as quickly as possible. Besides, she thought, if Charley had more people around him, he might feel better. She gathered her family and informed them that she planned to relocate to Englee.

THE PRICE PAID FOR CHARLEY

"You can start packing right now," she said in a tone that disallowed any argument.

The girls were pleased, but her sons, who cut wood for a living, were not. Although they said nothing, Fanny knew that they were disappointed. If their mother moved to Englee, they would have to fend for themselves. Joe had argued about Charley's attending his father's funeral, but he had been outnumbered. The boy appeared to have caught a cold at the ceremony, so now for his brother's sake Joe gave in to his mother's wishes again, approving the move to Englee.

Before daylight Wednesday the sleds were loaded with household supplies. Some residents of Englee had provided a few dogs to make up a second team, and much to Fanny's delight, later in the morning they had returned with four more dog teams for the trip.

"Mother," said Joe, "did you check the stovepipes before you lit the fire?"

"Oh, yes," Fanny said. "There were ten or so women at the house when I left, so don't worry about anything. Just get Charley ready for the trip. We'll have to put him in the coach box."

"He's very sick. By rights we should be taking him to St. Anthony."

Fanny sighed. "I doubt if he could stand the trip, Joe. It'll be hard enough to go to Englee."

"We'll take it steady, Mother," Joe promised. "I'll haul him myself. I'll put you and Charley in the coach box. There'll be no problem." All of Charley's brothers loved him dearly, but Joe possessed a compassionate streak unlike any other. He was a quiet young man who had the soul of a poet. Although he didn't have much in the way of formal education, the young man always participated in local concerts, writing material which he then recited himself.

Fanny thought of Mark and his close call with death, and she thanked God that, despite the family's loss, at least he had been spared. At 2:00 p.m. she and her entire family left Roddickton and Skipper Jim behind. She looked toward the forest near the shoreline across the river, at the area where Jim had been buried, then down at Charley, who was asleep with his head on her lap.

"May everything turn out all right," she prayed.

Joe cracked the whip and the dogs took off, headed for Englee and whatever awaited them.

Three weeks went by and saw no noticeable improvement in Charley's condition. The Hancock family were only beginning to accept the loss of Skipper Jim, but now they faced the very real possibility that their youngest boy would slip away as well.

Fanny helped Charley across the kitchen to the table one stormy morning in mid-February. Unable to walk on his own, he cried out in pain each time he was moved. Seeing him suffer like this broke her heart.

We should have taken him to St. Anthony like Joe said, she thought.

She seated him and placed two slices of toasted bread in front of him. "Charley, do you feel any better?" she asked. Her tone of voice demanded an honest answer.

THE PRICE PAID FOR CHARLEY

Charley put a hand to his forehead. "No, Mother," he said, his voice trembling with weakness. Despite his effort to spare her more concern (and he had tried, the best he could manage being a quivering squeak), Charley's pain came through again, and this time he cried out.

His mother sighed, resolving to be firm. Fanny squared her jaw and said, "Well, Charley, it's time we did something more to help you."

He stared blankly. "What are you going to do, Mother?"

"I'm going to send for Dr. Grenfell."

Charley almost fell out of his chair. His mind conjured the image of a scalpel cutting into his flesh. "No, Mother!" he pleaded. "I'll be all right." His fear of sharp instruments was greater than his fear of his illness.

"I'm sending for the doctor, Charley!" Fanny repeated. "As soon as the storm is over. This has gone far enough."

Charley couldn't eat much at the best times. Now the thought of eating was out of the question. He just stared at his food in terrified silence, his heart hammering in his chest.

"Charley, the doctor will make you better."

"I'm scared, Mother."

So am I, Charley, she thought, but kept her peace.

6

DR. WILFRED GRENFELL'S DREAM was to introduce reindeer to the Great Northern Peninsula. While with the Mission to Deep Sea Fishermen, he became familiar with Norway's reindeer herds. The experience sparked an idea for a similar operation along the coast of Labrador and on Newfoundland's Great Northern Peninsula. While in northern Norway he visited a tannery. He knew the state of the seal fishery around northern Newfoundland and in Labrador, so he ambitiously planned to build a tannery and craft industry in the north, and sell the product to the United States. His American bankers had conducted a study to investigate Newfoundland's environmental suitability for a reindeer herd, and ascertained that it would be a worthwhile but expensive endeavour. They promised to finance half of the cost; Dr. Grenfell would be responsible to raise the remainder. The Newfoundland government flatly refused to support the doctor and his hospital, and thus it came as a surprise when millionaires around New York and Boston became excited at the prospect and financed his part of the project.

THE PRICE PAID FOR CHARLEY

In addition to having superior medical skills, Dr. Grenfell was a master self-promoter and salesman. Travelling to England he had met with Anglo-Newfoundland Development Company officials and outlined his intentions. He emphasized the benefits the new species would bring to the company's Newfoundland branch. One could be self-sufficient in meat, milk, cheese, butter, and cooking oil. One could manufacture skin-boots for men in the bush, leather for horses' harnesses, and hair for mattresses in the logging camps.

Furthermore, he planned to use the animals in place of horses to transport men and materials to the lumber camps. Reindeer could haul pulpwood to the lakes and rivers in the winter, and in the spring they could be turned loose on the barrens. There would be no cost of feeding them in the summer. The English doctor had delivered a stirring speech, and the shareholders had bought the package. His dream had come true.

On the afternoon of Monday, January 6, the sound of a steamer's whistle caught the attention of the children in St. Anthony. The ship announcing its arrival was the 2,000-ton Norwegian freighter *Anita*. The steamer had arrived behind schedule after a mass of ice in Notre Dame Bay had prevented off-loading at Lewisporte. A backup plan was then implemented for the captain to touch in at St. Anthony.

A captain unfamiliar with ice would not take any unnecessary risks, especially far from home. The skipper of the *Anita* had become unnerved when he watched the ice carry south along the Great Northern Peninsula by the Arctic current, tearing loose solid granite and groaning threateningly as it went. After several days of floundering in the shifting, winding ice, the *Anita* stuck in a thick icefield, tossing in the mighty swell half a mile from Crémaillère. So the captain, with little consideration for human or animal, was ready to dump his cargo at the nearest port. Three hundred reindeer, reindeer moss, four Laplander families, dogs, and supplies made up his cargo.

The captain viewed the 600-foot cliffs through a veil of drifting snow kicked up by the strong northeast wind. He could not enter St. Anthony's harbour because of ice pressure, but now he found himself near the entrance of a small cove at the base of some imposing cliffs. He ordered the mate to keep blowing the whistle. The chart showed St. Anthony to be only three miles away. Once a French fishing village in the 1700s, the town carried a familiar name. In the year 1900, Dr. Wilfred Grenfell had chosen St. Anthony for his hospital and the headquarters for his medical centre, the International Grenfell Association.

The *Anita*'s captain issued a decisive order to his crew. "Get those animals and Laps off this ship, or I'm taking them back to Norway!"

The crew turned to see people waving frantically on the shore. The captain thought they were signalling him on to St. Anthony. Since he had no intention of going there, he ignored them and prepared to land in the cove.

The onlookers were surprised to see the ship in this location. Indeed, the boat was about to land on a shoal. They waved but could not gain the captain's attention. Noticing the gangway being lowered, they sent four experienced fishermen out to the ship. The heaving sea made navigating the ice a deadly gamble. The ship was now side on to the swell, and rolling dangerously. The four fishermen were met by a crewman who didn't speak English.

"Take us to the captain immediately!" one of the Newfoundlanders demanded.

Their request was understood, or at least guessed at, and they were taken to the bridge.

The fisherman who had addressed the ship's crew member stepped forward. "Captain, you are about to go upon a shoal!"

The skipper's eyes widened in disbelief.

"Go full speed ahead, Captain. You might get away from them."

The captain barked a command, and the *Anita* made a slow turn. Everyone looked overboard and saw breaking shoals to one side. Luckily the ship cleared them.

"Now turn your ship parallel to the land, Captain. You'll never unload in this position. Your ship is rolling too much."

The captain followed the Newfoundlander's instructions and succeeded in getting the ship to face the swell. The Laplander families disembarked first with their belongings. Unaccustomed to the dense ice so typical of the Newfoundland and Labrador winter, they stood shaking and frightened. They waited while the crew began the long and laborious task of unloading the animals and supplies.

Just after dark the ship struck a shoal, but miraculously she suffered no greater damage than a minor leak. By midnight the sea had worsened. After the last reindeer was led out of the boat, the captain bid the fishermen a hasty farewell and manoeuvred the *Anita* away from the shore and toward dry dock at Newfoundland's capital city, St. John's.

Sir Mason Beaton, head of the Grand Falls pulp and paper mill, received word that his reindeer had landed near St. Anthony. This was a problem. He would either have to leave the herd with Dr. Grenfell at St. Anthony all winter and transport them to Lewisporte the following summer by coastal boat, or he could drive the herd from St. Anthony down the Great Northern Peninsula and on to Millertown, at the head of the Exploits River on Red Indian Lake, where a holding corral had been constructed. At a meeting with his head staff to discuss their options, one person suggested scrapping the operation and donating the animals to Dr. Grenfell, but Beaton would not hear of it. He decided the reindeer would be driven from St. Anthony to Millertown, a distance of approximately four hundred miles of rough country.

The general manager of the AND Company set about forming a team to execute the plan. Beaton called Hugh Cole and Tom Greening into his office and outlined the task ahead. Hugh Cole was an Englishman who had come to Newfoundland in 1902 and now worked as an assistant to the surveyor with the company, Major Sullivan. Cole was tough and capable and knew his job well. He was familiar with maps and compass and the winter conditions in Newfoundland. His colleague, a Newfoundlander named Thomas Greening, worked with the company as a woods foreman. He was in top physical condition and possessed tremendous endurance.

The two men knew this was a massive undertaking, but they were both excited to be assigned to the operation. Hugh, although younger than Tom, was asked to supervise the venture. He gathered together the known maps of the Great Northern Peninsula and formed a strategy with his friends. They would leave St. Anthony with the reindeer herd sometime after the first of March, cross Hare Bay to Main Brook, take Dr. Grenfell's trail to Canada Bay, and follow Cloud River to the high country. Once they reached the open hills, however, they would need a guide to take them to Parson's Pond.

He offered the name of a friend, Mattie Mitchell, who was a Micmac Indian. Mitchell had come as a boy to Newfoundland from Nova Scotia and lived on St. John's Island near Port au Choix, on the west side of the Great Northern Peninsula. There he became a famous fur trapper. In 1906 Mitchell had gained instant fame as the prospector who discovered the Buchans ore deposit. Beaton, Cole, and Greening agreed that he was their best choice and immediately set about hiring him. Hugh and Tom agreed to rendezvous with Mitchell at Roddickton on Sunday, February 16.

Beaton ended the meeting with a stern lecture. "Maybe you're not aware of the importance of this project. The owners of the company in England, and the entire board of directors, are completely behind this enterprise. I'm ordered to advise everyone under my employ that they're to make sure that the project works. It'll mean the difference in making this paper company a success or a failure."

On Saturday, January 25, Hugh Cole and Tom Greening and their dogs left Millertown for Deer Lake by train. Twenty-two days out of Deer Lake, they arrived at Dr. Grenfell's sawmill at Roddickton and met with Mattie Mitchell. They stayed overnight at the cookhouse and left the next morning for St. Anthony.

After fighting a severe blizzard, the three men crossed Hare Bay and stayed for half a day with George Reid at Lock's Cove. George was a raw-boned and broad-shouldered man who was well respected in Ireland's Bight. He was also a gold mine of information, the kind of person who questioned everybody he met, young and old alike. If Ireland's Bight came up in a conversation, George Reid's name was sure to accompany it. He was not a lawyer, but everyone, including Dr. Grenfell, sought his advice in such matters.

Hugh reported an excellent mass of ice in Hare Bay and told George he wanted to drive their reindeer herd across it, thereby saving twenty-five miles of travelling around the bay. George warned him that the ice was unpredictable. One day it could be frozen hard enough to hold elephants, and the next one could cross it in a rowboat. You could be halfway across the bay and not make it to the other shore, since the sea could heave without warning and break up the ice underneath your feet.

"It's happened to me, son," George said to Hugh. Though he was young, Hugh was in charge, so George tried not to sound too condescending.

Hugh grinned. "Mr. Reid," he said, "there's one thing you

THE PRICE PAID FOR CHARLEY

can count on. Before I cross the bay, I'll be coming to talk with you first. I'll also be coming here to pick up my supplies. If I leave them here I won't have to haul them back from St. Anthony."

"You're right." George scratched his head. Maybe this young fellow knew what he was doing after all, he thought.

"Mr. Reid," Hugh continued, "have you any relatives at Roddickton or Englee?"

George was surprised. "No. Why do you ask?"

"Well, sir, I stopped at Dr. Grenfell's sawmill at Roddickton yesterday. There was a man there, a cutter. His name was Aaron Reid, your same last name. Let me tell you, he's quite a man."

"I know him quite well, but he's no relation to me." George, anxious for an explanation, said, "Carry on. What happened for him to impress you like that?"

"Aaron Reid told me one of the wildest stories I've ever heard in my life. I don't think I'll ever forget it. We stayed at the bunkhouse with the other men, and that's where Aaron told us about a man who drowned in January. But the story was about the drowned man's son, Mark, who was with him at the time.

"Mark was at the bunkhouse and introduced himself. Aaron said Mark had frozen to death, but that they thawed him out. Some old woman from Englee brought him back to life! Mark said the story wasn't exactly true since he hadn't really died, but he showed us his toenails, which were just starting to grow back. If it's only half true, the story and Mark's picture should go in papers all over the world."

"I know the story," George said thoughtfully, "and it's true. Aaron Reid told me himself, sitting right where you are now."

"What do you think of it, Mr. Reid?" Hugh asked.

"I believe it. There were a lot of people there to witness it."

Hugh nodded. He looked over at his companions, then snapped his fingers. "Oh yes! I have a message to deliver to Dr. Grenfell."

"What would that be, now?" George grinned.

"He's needed immediately in Englee. Mark's youngest brother, Charley, is sick. In fact, he's too ill to move, and a request has been made for Dr. Grenfell to go there right away. Aaron and Mark were just about to leave for St. Anthony, so we promised them that we'd deliver the message."

"You can't go in this blizzard, boys," George said as Hugh and the others rose to leave.

Hugh raised his voice slightly and called out in his thick English accent, "Thanks for the tea, Mrs. Reid." He shook hands with George and said, "I'll be coming in on the way back."

Hugh, Tom, and Mattie left the warmth of the Reid house and marched into the drifting snow. They were soon forced to spend the night in an abandoned house farther up in Ireland's Bight, however, when the blizzard came on stronger. The next day was blustery as they arrived at St. Anthony, and they went directly to Dr. Grenfell's hospital. Hugh reported Charley Hancock's worsening condition to the nurse on duty, patiently answering the woman's questions about the boy in Englee. He said he would like to make an appointment to see Dr. Grenfell. The nurse said he could see him right away, as the doctor had been expecting him for some time. Thanking her, Hugh found his way into Dr. Grenfell's office.

"So, you have come for fifty reindeer, Hugh."

Dr. Wilfred Grenfell looked up from the file he was examining. He was a handsome man with a neatly groomed mustache, and his gentle English accent sounded musical to the young man.

"Yes, sir," Hugh replied politely.

"Very well. I'll have Colonel Lindsay separate your reindeer from ours." Lindsay was a tough Irishman who had gotten his title from his position as chief of police in the city of Dublin. He emigrated to the colony of Newfoundland, at Dr. Grenfell's behest, to establish and train a law enforcement unit to protect the reindeer from poachers. He would spend most of the winter of 1908 in a tent on the White Hills only to discover that Newfoundlanders did not jump when he cracked his whip. Discouraged, he would take the first opportunity to exit this godforsaken place and never return.

"Okay," said Hugh.

"In the meantime," the doctor continued, leaning back in his chair, "I'll be going to Englee to check on this Hancock boy you mentioned. Did they say how long he's been sick?"

"Not exactly, sir, but I think it's been about a month or so."

"All right. You can stay at the annex, all three of you. I will see you in a couple of days."

Dr. Grenfell rang the bell on his desk, and a nurse

appeared. "Have Mr. Cole and his party shown to their quarters in the annex," he said, and just as Hugh was being led away, he added, "Mr. Cole, one moment, please. Did you come across Hare Bay?"

"Yes, I did, sir."

"And how is the ice?"

"It's excellent, perhaps a foot thick. We put a couple of holes through, and it's very solid."

"Good," Dr. Grenfell said and stood up. "That's the way I will be taking, then. It should save a good hour's drive, should it not? It's a long way around that bay."

Hugh smiled, pleased that he had given this distinguished gentleman some sound advice. "I plan to drive our herd of reindeer across there as well," he said, "when we go."

The doctor turned to his nurse. "Get my instruments packed and ready," he said. "Put in everything I will need to perform an operation. It sounds like the boy may have a case of pemphigus."

He scribbled a note to explain his absence, which the nurse took and hurried off. The doctor then bid his guest farewell and continued his preparations for departure to Englee.

7

FANNY WAS WORRIED. Charley was unable to move, and she figured he was about to sink into a coma. She paced the floor, wondering if Dr. Grenfell was going to respond to her message. She voiced her thoughts to Mark, who sat at the table.

"Maybe Dr. Grenfell didn't get the message," she said. "Maybe the reindeer man forgot to pass the message along to the hospital."

Mark shook his head. "Dr. Grenfell will be here tomorrow, Mother. This fellow Hugh Cole can be trusted. If I didn't think he could be trusted, we'd have gone ourselves. There was an awful blizzard yesterday, too, so I'd say they had to stay at Lock's Cove all night."

"How do you know this man is as reliable as you say?" Fanny stopped pacing and looked straight at Mark. "How do you know?" she repeated, clenching her fists.

"Listen, Mother," Mark replied slowly, "Mr. Pomeroy knows this man well. He gave us a guarantee that our message was in safe hands. Also, Mother, Mattie Mitchell was with him, and we know him."

"You listen, Mark! You're putting Charley's life in the hands of an Indian."

Mark was becoming agitated. He tapped his finger on the table. "Mother," he said, "you have to calm down. Your mind is in a state where you don't trust anyone. Mattie has to go to the hospital himself. He has erysipelas on his face and I think he's in bad shape. Listen, he wouldn't put a case like Charley's second to anything, even his own, so don't worry. Dr. Grenfell will be here, and if not, Dr. Little."

Fanny sat down and blinked back tears. "I've had an awful winter, my son, ever since your father drowned. I don't know what's in store for us from one day to the next. Poor Charley is getting weaker and weaker, and if someone doesn't come tomorrow, I have a feeling it'll be too late."

Mark put a hand on his mother's shoulder. "I know you've had a hard year, but try to keep strong for Charley's sake."

"I'm trying," she replied, and walked to the bedroom where Charley lay delirious.

Later that evening Mark and his mother sat at the table, waiting for Aunts Lizzie and Emmie to come out of the room with their report on Charley. Soon the two women appeared and sat at the table. The water steamed in the kettle. Fanny placed a cup of tea before each of them.

"Aunt Lizzie," she said, "what can you tell us?"

The midwives gave each other an uneasy glance. "It's not what I thought it was all along," Aunt Lizzie began. "Charley

THE PRICE PAID FOR CHARLEY

has an abscess on the bone near his thigh. The only good thing about it is that it's below the joint, but it appears that it may have a touch of gangrene."

Aunt Emmie spoke up. "For goodness' sake, Aunt Fanny, why hasn't Charley been taken to St. Anthony? The boy is in severe pain, and if he doesn't receive an operation within the next forty-eight hours, it'll be too late. I can tell you now, it'll be a miracle if he doesn't lose his leg." Emmie Fillier, known as Aunt Emmie, was the unofficial mother of the east side of the Great Northern Peninsula. At eighteen years of age she had married Esau Fillier, who worked as a foreman at Dr. Grenfell's Roddickton sawmill. Although she had received no formal medical training, at nineteen she was equal to any registered nurse, according to Dr. Grenfell. She had received on-the-job training from the doctor himself and assisted in some of his operations at Englee.

Fanny put a weary hand to her forehead and looked at the older and more experienced Aunt Lizzie for encouragement.

"It seems that the infection is spreading to Charley's groin. He has a swollen gland under his right arm, which is a sign that he has blood poisoning. If Dr. Grenfell isn't here by tomorrow evening, we'll have to operate ourselves. We'll probably have to take his leg off, but that'll be done only as a last resort."

Fanny had known these women long enough to know when they were sincere and when they were exaggerating. Both of them bore the same expression, calm and serious.

Poor Charley, she thought. *Imagine sawing off the bone and saying goodbye to that crippled leg that I've cared for all*

these years. Suppose Charley doesn't survive the operation—suppose he is too weak to go through it!
　She started to cry.
　Aunt Lizzie Gillard was not only a midwife and a self-appointed nurse, but a counsellor as well. She took Fanny into her arms and let her cry.

In the early hours of the morning, after the two midwives had gone home after administering to Charley what care they could, Fanny called her sons and told them that Charley's condition had taken a turn for the worse. They jumped out of bed and bounded into his bedroom. Charley was white and still and at first glance appeared to be dead. Only the sound of his breathing registered life.
　Roy sat on the bed, put his hand on Charley's forehead, and brushed back his hair. Cold sweat stood out on the boy's brow. Charley opened his eyes and looked imploringly at Roy. The pity in the eyes of the fifteen-year-old was too much for Roy, who had become close to his brother after watching him on many occasions when their mother picked berries or worked in the gardens. He loved his younger brother, and this was too much to bear. Roy had seen only death in Charley's eyes. He left the room and went to the kitchen.
　"What've we been doing?" he asked. "For weeks now we've been waiting around here, twiddling our thumbs while Charley's been getting worse and worse and worse." He punctuated each *worse* with a tap of his fist on the table.
　"Just what are we, anyway?" he continued. "A bunch of

THE PRICE PAID FOR CHARLEY

cowards? Haven't we got any of the old man's blood in our veins? If Father had been here last week, he would've carried Charley to St. Anthony in his arms."

"You're right," Fanny mumbled.

Roy, ever the hot-tempered one, grew furious. "Look at us," he shouted. "We're all over two hundred pounds each, and we brag about what we can do, yet we're too low-lifed to take a poor, sick cripple to the hospital!" This time his fist struck the table hard and set the plates to rattling.

Joe folded his arms. "Charley has been in the care of Aunt Lizzie and Aunt Emmie," he said quietly, hoping to calm his brother. "They told us to wait for Dr. Grenfell. For all we know he could be caught in the same storm we are."

"Listen," Mark piped in, siding with Roy, "I don't know about those old midwives. All they mind is a bottle of bogbean or a pot of juniper roots. It's a wonder they haven't got half the people around here poisoned. And now their latest remedy is 'Wait until Dr. Grenfell comes.'"

Roy nodded emphatically.

Will stood up. "Let's get Charley ready and take him to St. Anthony ourselves!"

Mark waved a hand at his brother. "Tomorrow morning we'll go, even if this blizzard is still on. 'Twill make no difference to me."

"I'm with you," said Roy. Turning to Fanny he said, "Mother, get Charley ready. It's better for him to die on his way to the hospital than here surrounded by a group of men too scared to do anything!"

Fanny was caught up in Roy's excitement, but after a moment's consideration, her shoulders slumped and she shook her head. She warned the boys that Charley wouldn't last an hour if they moved him, especially on dog team.

"Mother, it's not the movement that we're worried about. It's the poison in his system. He's slowly dying in there," Mark said, motioning toward the bedroom. The dull light of the lamp outlined Charley's form in his bed. The only movement coming from him was the slow rise and fall of his chest as his breath came in laboured gasps.

"Listen!" Roy barked. "There's a raging storm on. Maybe this fellow Cole is still at Hare Bay, held up in a blizzard. He left Roddickton on Monday and this is Wednesday, and there's no sign of Dr. Grenfell yet. Now, Mother, I want you to get Charley ready to move to St. Anthony. We'll leave in the morning."

At six o'clock the next morning, Emmie Fillier arrived at the Hancock home to attend to Charley, whose eyes had rolled up to whites, and his breathing was coming shorter and quicker. She examined his leg and found it swollen from the ankle all the way to the thigh, where there were three large lumps. Charley's groin was also swollen, and a bright red streak travelled up his hip. She touched the lumps and Charley winced.

"This is where the problem is," she stated flatly. If Charley did not get something done today, she said, then he was likely done for. Aunt Emmie had doubts that he would make it to St. Anthony, but it had to be done, today. She walked into the

THE PRICE PAID FOR CHARLEY

kitchen, where the family sat immobile. "I'm going to Aunt Lizzie's house to have a talk with her," she said. "Before I go you can start getting Charley ready for a trip to St. Anthony. I know it's impossible to use a boat in this weather, so he'll have to go by sled. You know what kind of ride it'll be. Every bump on the hard snow will hurt Charley to the bone, so the coach box will have to be padded well. You can start with a feather bed."

"Don't worry about that," offered Roy. "We'll have the softest bed for Charley that has ever been made."

Dr. Grenfell stood with two of his nurses at the hospital's entrance in St. Anthony. They held his medical bag and other essential supplies, ready to be loaded into his sled box. A lot of snow had fallen and the weather was bitterly cold. He had lost two days to it and was well aware that he didn't have a moment to lose.

A man nearby stopped shovelling snow when he saw the doctor. He came over to the sled. "Dr. Grenfell," he said, "Reuben has returned from Flower's Cove. He'll be going with you now."

The doctor was delighted. Reuben Simms was his permanent dog team driver. He depended on Reuben's experience with dogs and the northern climate, knowing he was in good hands whenever he ventured on the barrens or the saltwater ice, sometimes even during storms at night.

"Reuben," Dr. Grenfell said with concern as his driver emerged from a shed, "There's a young crippled boy at Englee who needs medical attention immediately. He may very well be dying. His father drowned in January while trying to get medicine for his boy, and Hugh Cole and his men risked their lives a couple of days ago, travelling in a blizzard to get here with the message. In fact, Hugh has frozen his face, and Mattie Mitchell, his hands and feet. It's up to us now to push right through to Englee without stopping."

Above the barking of the dogs and the excited murmur of people gathered around, Reuben declared, "Don't worry, Doctor, we'll get there."

Dr. Grenfell stepped aboard the sled and sat down, holding the rope in front of him to keep his balance. The chain drug that restrained the dogs was released, and the animals shot out of St. Anthony with Reuben and the English doctor in tow.

By two o'clock in the afternoon, the storm settled enough to permit a party, made up of Emmie Fillier, Fanny Hancock, ten men, and three dog teams, to start their arduous journey to St. Anthony, seventy miles away. Aunt Emmie and Fanny drove in the forward dog teams. The snow was deep and in places packed hard, but the two head dog teams moved with little effort. Mark was driving Charley's team behind them at a slower pace, taking care not to let the dogs hit too many bumps along the way. Charley was heavily padded and wrapped warmly in the accompanying coach box. Behind his sled, helpers walked along on snowshoes.

By three-thirty the travellers reached the bottom of Bide Arm, the halfway point to Roddickton. The lead teams stopped

THE PRICE PAID FOR CHARLEY

and waited for Charley's team to catch up. When he did Aunt Emmie climbed out and carefully examined the sick boy. He was restless and in intense pain.

"I'm too warm," he whispered.

Charley had had a high fever before he left home, but now, cooped up in the wooden box with the blankets around him, he felt like he was boiling. Aunt Emmie instructed a couple of men to tilt the coach box and fan Charley in order to stall his fever.

The snow lay two feet deep between Bide Arm and Roddickton, so when the trailing men on snowshoes caught up, they moved ahead of the teams to tramp down a trail for the dogs. It was a gruelling task, but by five o'clock, just as the sun touched the Cloud Hills, Charley's party arrived at Roddickton. They went immediately to the Hancocks' log cabin, which was partly drifted over with snow. Two men who were cutting logs for Dr. Grenfell were using the cabin as a winter camp, so it was accessible and thankfully had a supply of dry wood. Mark sent a dog team to Dr. Grenfell's mill to alert Aaron Reid that, if the doctor arrived, he should be advised that Charley was now at Roddickton.

The boy was in hard shape. When his companions removed him from the coach box, they were distressed to see that he was barely breathing. He lost consciousness as they brought him inside, and they tried to rouse him, but to no avail. They laid him on the kitchen couch and waited while the women moved in and lit the lamp. Aunt Emmie determined that Charley could not be moved any farther. His pulse was irregular and his temperature too high.

EARL B. PILGRIM

"I'm sure that Dr. Grenfell is on his way here," she declared. "It's the snow that has delayed him. He'll be here."

The nineteen-year-old midwife turned and said, "Roy, here's what you should do. Get some men and one of the dog teams, and send them to meet Dr. Grenfell."

"They've already gone, Emmie," Roy said bitterly. "This should've been done two weeks ago."

Outside the men looked up from their tea and bread at the sound of barking dogs. They looked to their own dogs, which were milling around in a calm, disinterested fashion. One of the men shouted to those inside, "Someone's coming! Hey! Someone's coming!"

Mark jumped to the window. A dog team approached, the same team he had sent on in advance. The driver was Allan Hancock, the young man who had covered Skipper Jim's body with the punt against the cold. He informed them that Dr. Grenfell had arrived.

8

FANNY DEMANDED THAT THE men leave the house. "Go out to the woodhouse," she said. "There's a stove out there. Dr. Grenfell is not going to operate on Charley with half of Roddickton staring over his shoulder."

"My jingles, Mother, calm down," said Mark. "We've got that taken care of. We've got the fire going in the shed."

"Good. Then please leave, now." She turned to Aunt Emmie, the young midwife. "Emmie, what do you think?" Fanny was nervous about meeting the English doctor she'd heard so much about. She was afraid she wouldn't know what to say.

"Take it easy, Aunt Fanny. Dr. Grenfell will be here in a few minutes. Don't get excited. He's only a man."

"Mother." The voice was low.

Fanny looked over to see Charley prop himself up on one elbow. She went to him and urged him to lie down, putting her arm around him for comfort. "Lie down, my son. Dr. Grenfell will be here any moment."

Charley looked around, surprised. "Mother, we're back home in Roddickton. If only Father were here . . ." He fell back on his pillow.

"Don't worry about anything," Aunt Emmie consoled. "Dr. Grenfell is coming, and you'll be better in no time."

"Will he take my leg, Mother?"

"Why, no, Charley," the midwife said before Fanny could reply. "The most he'll do is open the infected places."

Charley closed his eyes.

"He's here!" shouted Fanny.

The two women smoothed their long white aprons and opened the door. A dog team had stopped outside, and a man dressed in a fur coat moved confidently toward the doorway.

"Good evening, ladies." It was a stately voice, with a crisp English accent that sounded exotic to the women's ears.

"Good evening, Dr. Grenfell," said Aunt Emmie.

The doctor stepped inside and ignited the gaslight for the mantle lamp he'd obtained from Ishmael Pomeroy, the manager of his sawmill. He'd stopped there briefly to retrieve the light, for it would come in handy during what he expected to be a lengthy operation.

"This is Aunt Fanny Hancock, Charley's mother," Emmie said.

"How do you do?" asked Dr. Grenfell, smiling. He was a fine-looking man with a charismatic demeanour. "I heard of your great loss this winter, and for this I am very sorry."

Fanny stammered, humbled by this distinguished gentleman. "Thank you," she managed.

THE PRICE PAID FOR CHARLEY

"I understand you are very worried about your son Charley. May I see him?"

Fanny grinned in spite of herself. Of course he could! Aunt Emmie led the doctor toward Charley.

"May I have a chair, please?" the doctor asked politely. Fanny brought him a chair, and he sat near Charley. Turning his attention to the sick teenager, he asked softly, "How are you, Charley?"

Charley only nodded his head and stared with glassy eyes at the man before him.

The doctor placed his hand on the boy's forehead and asked, "How old are you, Charley?"

"Fifteen."

"I hear you can read and write. You should be very proud of that. If you have to go to the St. Anthony hospital, you will be going to school every day you're there."

Charley smiled, and his mother felt a sudden surge of love for her son. It was the first time she had seen him smile since his father died.

"Put out your tongue," Dr. Grenfell said. His young patient complied. The doctor used his light and looked down Charley's throat, and then into his eyes. He took out an instrument and measured the boy's heartbeat, blood pressure, pulse.

"Where do you find the pain, Charley?"

"In my leg, Doctor."

"Okay. I'm going to take a look at it, so you just try to take it easy."

Charley nodded weakly while the doctor slowly pulled back the bedclothes.

"I notice Charley is wearing a suit of woollen underwear," he observed. "Could you please remove them for me?"

"Yes, Doctor," Aunt Emmie said.

Dr. Grenfell walked to the cupboard and picked up a sugar bowl. Antique, he observed. He turned at the sound of Charley groaning.

"Okay, Doctor," Aunt Emmie called from the boy's bedside.

When he returned to Charley and pulled down the blanket, he immediately diagnosed the problem. Charley's leg and part of his groin were in the advanced stages of infection.

"Charley has osteomyelitis, an inflammation of the bone marrow." Grenfell leaned forward, now touching the infected leg. Charley whimpered in pain.

"Young man, you have a large tubercle on your leg, but I'll see what I can do."

The doctor pulled the bedclothes back over his patient and went to the other side of the room, to Fanny. "Mrs. Hancock," he said, "Charley has a very serious infection on his femur, the big bone of his leg. It's about six inches above his knee. It is life-threatening without treatment, so we will have to intervene right away. I'll have to open his leg and clean it here tonight. I would prefer to do this at the hospital, of course, but I can manage here."

The colour had drained from Fanny's face.

"Don't worry," the doctor said, and smiled, laying a comforting hand on her shoulder. "I'll do what I can, Mrs. Hancock."

"Okay, okay, Doctor," she said without any hesitation, placing all of her faith in him.

THE PRICE PAID FOR CHARLEY

"Are the rest of your family here?"

Aunt Emmie spoke up. "Yes, Doctor. Three of her sons are in the shed."

"Tell them I want to see them."

"Okay, Doctor," she said, and she went to call them.

Mark, Roy, and Joe entered the house. They were all healthy, burly men. Mark was easily the biggest, at 230 pounds. Dr. Grenfell shook hands with each of the brothers.

"Gentlemen," he said, all business, "Charley has a bone infection called osteomyelitis. He has a large tubercle about six inches above his knee. I have to make an incision to drain the infection, and it has to be done here tonight. If it is not done now, he will not live much longer. Your mother has given me permission to operate, however, I thought it important to talk with you also before I went ahead."

The three brothers looked from one to the other.

"If you want, please talk with your mother before you make a decision," he concluded.

The boys offered no argument, so the doctor nodded and went to work at once.

A woollen blanket was placed on the table and a white sheet over that. It was a simple task for the three brothers to lift the frail boy to the makeshift operating table, heartbreaking though it was to visualize Charley being cut open. Each of them fought back tears as they laid him out on the table. Fanny cradled Charley's head as they nudged him to the middle, then she slipped a pillow beneath him when he was in place. The three brothers gave their mother a solemn look and turned to leave.

"Just a minute, men," said Dr. Grenfell. "I want you to stay a moment longer. I'm going to pray to God that He will help me perform this operation, and that He will help Charley recover speedily. Do you mind?"

The brothers stood around the English doctor, and each bent his head in prayer.

"Dear Lord," Dr. Grenfell began in a low voice, "You know about the operation that I am about to perform. I want You to guide my hand and make it steady. I want You to make this operation a success. And I want You to help these men to realize that Charley will be among them tomorrow. We ask all these things of You. Amen."

His words were soothing to the Hancock family, lightening the burden. Following the benediction, the three brothers went out and Fanny shut the door.

"Emmie."

"Yes, Doctor?"

"Would you please sterilize these instruments for me?"

"Yes, Doctor." The young midwife took the instruments Dr. Grenfell had wrapped in a heavy white cloth, and placed them in a pot of scalding water.

"Okay, Emmie. Let us take a closer look." He uncovered the young man's leg from the thigh down, exposing the swollen areas. *What pain this young lad must be enduring*, he thought.

"How do you feel, Charley?" he asked.

"Very good," Charley replied nervously.

"You will not feel a thing while I operate."

The boy nodded.

THE PRICE PAID FOR CHARLEY

"Emmie, I want you to shave Charley's leg for me, please." Aunt Emmie dampened the young man's leg with a wet gauze, swabbing it a few times with warm water to prepare for shaving.

"How does that feel?" the doctor asked.

Charley gave a feeble smile. "Pretty good."

Emmie took a soft brush and a straight razor, and gently removed the hairs from Charley's leg while the doctor rechecked his pulse. He knew Charley was undernourished and extremely weak, but he had no doubt that he would survive the operation. Fighting infection afterward would be the biggest challenge.

Dr. Grenfell opened a journal and wrote in it for a few minutes. He extracted some pills from a small vial and gave one to the young man. "Charley," he said reassuringly, "I'm going to give you chloroform. There will be a mask over your nose and mouth for just a minute, and when it touches your nose, you take a deep breath. I guarantee it won't hurt you. Okay, Charley?"

The doctor outlined to Aunt Emmie where he would make the incision. He examined Charley's knee joint closer, offering a silent prayer that it was free from infection. He pressed the bone below the knee. Charley whimpered in response.

"I would say that the infection has reached the bone, or close to it," Dr. Grenfell said. "Anyhow, I will take a look."

He attached a strap to the table and tightened it across Charley's chest. He reached for the chloroform mask, and bending near Charley he said in a near whisper, "Now, Charley,

I am going to put this over your mouth, so don't be afraid. It won't hurt you. Make sure you take a deep breath, and count to ten."

The boy only nodded.

Emmie held Charley's head while Dr. Grenfell applied the mask. The boy breathed deeply, gave a weak grunt, and fell limp.

"Okay, Emmie, you keep an eye on his heartbeat."

Now that he could examine the patient more thoroughly, the doctor moved to Charley's leg and pushed gently on the large protuberance above the knee. Next he swabbed the leg with alcohol. Gripping his scalpel, he made a small incision. He paused to make another notation in his book, then drained pus from the infected area, enough to fill several vials. With the pressure now released, he was able to open the incision some more and dig deeper. He incised further to expose the bone, then pointed out his findings to Emmie.

"This is very serious," Dr. Grenfell said, "but it can be cured if drained properly."

Emmie nodded, her eyes wide with nervous curiosity.

"If we had him at the hospital, I would get a better look at the bone, but our problem here now is the light," the doctor said.

He and Emmie set about cleaning the infected areas of Charley's leg as Fanny paced to and fro in the next room, fearing for her youngest son as he lay unaware with his eyes closed, looking for all the world like a dead man. Her thoughts were echoed by the boys in the shed as they paced nervously. Roy felt uneasy and more than a little guilty. Imagine, putting your brother on a table to be butchered by an Englishman! No matter how many people spoke highly of Dr. Grenfell, he hadn't yet proven himself to the Hancock brothers. He was just a doctor with a dream. A couple of times, Mark's impatience and anxiety got the best of him, and he threatened to go into the house.

"Suppose he's got Charley killed," he blurted.

"Don't be foolish, Mark," Roy chided. "There's one thing for sure—he can't do more damage than we've already done."

II

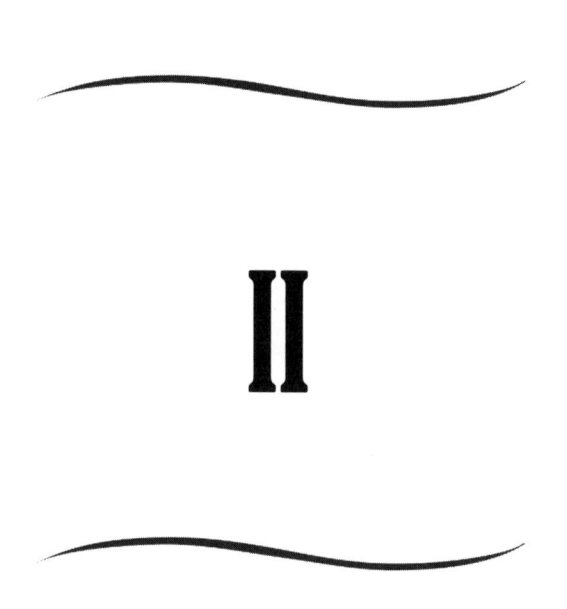

9

DR. GRENFELL CLOSED THE incision in Charley's leg about two-thirds and instructed Emmie to leave it open to allow for draining. Some colour was coming back into the boy's face. Two hours had passed since he went under. Dr. Grenfell passed Emmie a small bottle and continued with his instructions. "The patient is undernourished and will have to take these vitamins," he said.

"Yes, Doctor, I will give them to him."

"We have only a few more minutes before he awakens, so let's clean up this mess."

As they were cleaning up, Charley came around and became nauseous, then vomited. The doctor gave him a painkiller, then called Charley's mother, who bolted into the room almost as soon as the words left the doctor's mouth. Her eyes were swollen and red, and she looked exhausted.

"How is he, Doctor?"

Dr. Grenfell smiled reassuringly. "His problem is not all that rare, Mrs. Hancock," he said. "He can be well soon with proper care."

Fanny walked over to her boy. She cupped his face in her hands and stared at him, surprised to see him awake already. Only a few minutes earlier, she had been almost certain that he was dead, because it had taken the doctor so long to call her. She blew out a relieved sigh. "Thank God you're all right, Charley."

"No need to worry, Mrs. Hancock," Dr. Grenfell said. "We'll have to move him to the bedroom, though, because he won't be able to travel anytime soon."

"Mark and the boys will have to come in and give us a hand," Aunt Emmie said.

She called the young men from the shed and they rushed in, identical expressions of anxiety on their faces.

"How is he?" Roy asked, his eyes darting to Charley and the white sheet covering him. His eyes widened when he saw his younger brother shift on the table. Charley was moaning and urging to throw up.

"He's fine. A bit groggy, but he'll do fine," the doctor said. "Gentlemen, your brother needs your help to get him to the bedroom. After that's done, I want to talk with you.

Charley seemed weightless as his brothers slipped their hands under him and hoisted him into the air. They carried him with ease to his bedroom and placed him on the wooden bed. They excused themselves and looked on curiously as Dr. Grenfell wedged himself between them and the bed, hooking up an intravenous to his patient. He then went into the kitchen with the boys in tow, where Fanny was sitting at the table. She stood and prepared a mug of tea for the doctor.

"Thank you, Mrs. Hancock," he said, and sat down. He stirred in some sugar and tasted his tea. Nodding in approval, Dr. Grenfell looked up at the Hancock boys and said, "Which one of you is the eldest son?"

"I am," Roy said.

"Well, Roy, I want to tell you something about Charley's condition. When I opened up his leg, I confirmed what I suspected. Osteomyelitis is a bacterial infection of the bone marrow, and very painful. It causes abscesses to form, and these discharge pus. Charley had three of these abscesses, and they were ready to discharge, but I opened his leg and cleaned it up.

"Your brother was fortunate that it hadn't gotten into the knee joint. We have to be very careful at this stage, because if it gets into the joint, it will kill the bone in his leg. If that happens, the bone will have to come out, and that means amputation. He is going to have quite a battle to fight off infection.

"I found Charley to be very undernourished, and I suspect his iron is very low. His heart rate was slow, so he didn't lose a lot of blood during the operation. Now, here's what will happen. I intend to leave the lower part of the operation open, to allow any infections to drain out."

The boys looked wide-eyed at Dr. Grenfell. This was the first time they had been in the presence of a medical doctor, and they were overwhelmed by what he was saying. After giving his brothers a confused look, Roy said, "Doctor, I don't know what these big words mean, but there are a couple of questions I'd like to ask."

"Go ahead."

"We've been saying all along that Charley has a TB leg." All too often, such a diagnosis was a death sentence. "Does he have TB?"

"I definitely did not find any in Charley's operation, but if he doesn't get the proper care, it is possible that his leg could develop tuberculosis."

"Doctor," Roy continued, "what are his chances of surviving here in this log cabin, compared to the hospital at St. Anthony?"

"Charley can survive this operation anywhere, as long as he doesn't get another cold or a chill, and if he is given the medicine and vitamins that I'm going to prescribe. I'll be leaving him in charge of Emmie and Mrs. Elizabeth Gillard, but he will have to stay here for at least three weeks before he can be moved back home."

Roy nodded, and for once the excitable young man was speechless.

"Which one of you was in the water with your father?"

Mark stepped forward.

Dr. Grenfell gave the young man an appraising look. "Do you have any problems with your hands or feet?" he asked.

"No, Doctor."

"Amazing." The doctor shook his head in disbelief, clearly astounded at Mark's recovery.

"Mark," the English doctor said, "what you went through is nothing short of superhuman. I've heard the stories. Charley is from the same bloodline as you, so I am sure he will survive the operation."

Mark nodded, though he wasn't sure that his own strength had been given to Charley as well. "You know, I would have lost my hands if it wasn't for Aunt Lizzie."

"Is that so?"

"I couldn't feel a thing, but she dipped my hands in some buckets of cold water. The feeling came back, then . . . and talk about pain! My jingles!"

The doctor stared at him, fascinated. He looked at the young man's rough hands, then once again shook his head in amazement at what surely had been a miraculous recovery.

"The operation has been a success," he said, standing up, "but you can help the healing process by giving Charley lots of love, and praying for him night and day."

He laid a comforting hand on Mark's shoulder and went to the bedroom to check on his patient. He returned a few moments later and sat back down to a fresh cup of tea.

"Hugh Cole and the others," the doctor said, chuckling, "the three of them almost went over a cliff and into the sea the other night, trying to get word to St. Anthony. Only for the Micmac Indian, Mattie Mitchell, they would have drowned or frozen to death."

Mark grinned at the doctor's easygoing nature. "We knew something was wrong when you didn't show up sooner. That was why we decided to take him to St. Anthony today."

"Why hadn't you taken him there before?" Dr. Grenfell asked.

The brothers glanced toward the bedroom door, then at the doctor, but said nothing.

"Okay," he said, "tell my driver that I'll be going to the sawmill in about an hour's time."

The next morning the doctor returned to see Charley. He found the area he'd operated on was swollen, but draining well. The pain in Charley's leg had eased, and he had slept for a solid five hours. Emmie had given him a glass of orange juice and a bowl of porridge the doctor had provided. Overall he was pleased with his patient's condition.

"Now, Emmie," he insisted, "make sure the incision is left open. It will leave a scar, but that's a small price to pay, isn't it?"

Aunt Emmie smiled and shook hands with the English doctor.

"I'll be going back to St. Anthony today. It's up to you now. You can take the stitches out in about ten days. Just make sure Charley is in good condition before he is taken to Englee."

The midwife assured him Charley would be taken care of. Turning to his patient, Dr. Grenfell said, "Charley, if you obey the nurse and your mother and get lots of rest, you can be well in a very short time. Make sure you take your medicine, and get lots of bedrest."

"Yes, Doctor."

"Now, smile for me, Charley."

Charley forced a weak smile.

"That's it, Charley."

The doctor walked out with the young midwife close behind.

"Emmie," Dr. Grenfell cautioned, "We're going to have to be very careful with Charley. If there is any change for the worse, contact me immediately and we'll arrange to transport him to St. Anthony." He handed her a package of carbolic acid to be used as a disinfectant. "I'll be going back now, so tell John Wilcox that I will be writing him soon. And say hello to Elizabeth Gillard for me."

He was about to walk to his dogsled, but he turned in midstride.

"I almost forgot," he said, opening his bag and extracting a surgical knife. It was the fold-up type, with an ivory handle. He handed it to Emmie.

"This is for you. I want you to keep it as a souvenir from me. Use it for operations, if need be."

Aunt Emmie accepted the gift and promised she would always cherish it. Sudden tears welled in her eyes. She was touched that there were such kind men in the world. She wiped at her eyes as the handsome English doctor departed, en route to his hospital office at St. Anthony.

After the prescribed rest in the log cabin at Roddickton, Charley was well enough to go back to Englee. Two of his brothers, Mark and Joe, put him aboard a sled and hauled it the ten-mile distance to Englee. The trek home put the three Hancock boys in good spirits.

On Sunday, March 15, Dr. John Mason Little from Dr. Grenfell's hospital in St. Anthony arrived by dog team to examine the boy. Dr. Little was a young American who, fascinated by Dr. Grenfell's daring medical adventures, had come to the coast. He found Charley in fair condition, but, as Dr. Grenfell had already observed, undernourished. He had gained some weight, but some of the infection persisted. The physician ordered more medicine and advised Charley to rest, reiterating almost as an afterthought to his caregivers Dr. Grenfell's instructions to keep him warm.

The American doctor held a clinic, after which he spent the night with John Wilcox, the game warden, whom Dr. Grenfell considered a close friend. The following morning Dr. Little met Hugh Cole and his reindeer herd at Lane's Pond, midway between Roddickton and Main Brook. After lunch with Hugh and the others, the doctor continued his homeward journey to St. Anthony, following the trail set down by the reindeer. On Hugh's advice, he avoided crossing Hare Bay. The ice was not stable, and the doctor knew well the story of Skipper Jim Hancock and his son Mark.

On Tuesday evening a dog team pulling two men arrived at Englee. In the centre of town, the driver hailed a couple of men and asked for the location of Mark Hancock's house. One of the men pointed to a group of three houses, about half a mile away.

"One of them is Mark's," he advised.

Thanking the men, the visitors sped off in that direction. As they neared, the noise from the dogs alerted the people in the three houses. Their doors opened and people came out to find out what the commotion was.

Roy Hancock walked over to meet the newcomers. "Good day, gentlemen," he said.

THE PRICE PAID FOR CHARLEY

"Good day, sir," said one of the men. "We're looking for Mark Hancock. Can you tell us where he lives?"

"I sure can. I'm his brother Roy. Come to the house."

They secured their dogs and followed Roy into his house. Mark was sitting at the kitchen table, making new dog harnesses.

"Well," the young man said when he saw the newcomers, "if it isn't Hugh Cole and Mattie Mitchell." Mark put down his rope and knife, and shook hands with them. "Roy," he said, "meet Hugh and Mattie."

Roy shook their hands. "I've heard about you! We're grateful for what you did," he gushed.

Hugh and Mattie were then introduced to Fanny Hancock, who welcomed them with open arms.

"We came to see Charley," said Hugh.

Roy grinned. "Hey, Charley!" he called.

A voice from another room returned, "Yes, Roy, what is it?"

"Come out! There's someone here to see you."

"Who is it?"

"Come and see for yourself!"

"Do I know them?"

"No, but they're here to see you."

"Oh," said the voice, curiously.

The thump of wood on wood was heard coming from the bedroom. As the door opened, the frail, twisted frame of Charley Hancock appeared, dressed in oversized clothes and hobbling toward them on homemade crutches. The young man wore trousers that were too long, rolled at the legs and supported by suspenders. He shot a surprised look at the strangers, followed by a broad smile.

"So, you're Charley, are you?" Hugh said in his rich English accent.

Charley peered at the man, looking into his soft eyes. A life spent in the Badger logging camps had made Hugh Cole a tough and rugged-looking man, but he had a tender heart, and emotion showed in his eyes now. His strong hand reached out to shake Charley's.

"How do you do, Mr. Cole?"

"I am fine," said Hugh. "How are you?"

"I am very good, sir."

"I'm glad." Hugh's voice cracked as he spoke. "Charley," he said, "I want you to meet my friend." He pointed to the woodsman standing beside him. "This is Mattie Mitchell."

Charley's eyes widened. Ever since Mark came back from Roddickton where he and his brothers had first met Hugh Cole and Mattie Mitchell at the sawmill, there had been a lot of talk in Englee about this man with the high cheekbones and jet-black hair. *A real Indian*, Charley thought. This was beyond his wildest dreams! Indians were mysterious people who were respected as great woodsmen and hunters.

Mattie walked over and gave Charley a firm handshake. Though he had spent most of his life roaming the hills and barrens, he was a family man who found it difficult not to feel for Charley. "Charley," he said, "I'm glad to meet you. Dr. Grenfell told us how you came through your operation. He said you were very tough."

THE PRICE PAID FOR CHARLEY

Charley beamed with pride.

Hugh cleared his throat. "Charley," he said, "do you know that Mattie is a real Indian? But don't worry, he won't be scalping anyone while we're in town."

Everyone roared with laughter. Mark laughed until tears came, and he wiped at his eyes and motioned for the men to sit down. His mother and his sister, Dellah, prepared lunch for the visitors as Roy helped Charley to the table.

When Charley was seated and made comfortable, Joe smiled at Hugh and Mattie. "We know you risked your lives to get to the doctor in that terrible storm," he said.

"We did only what any normal person would have done, and we're happy to have done it," Hugh said.

"Thank you very much. How can we ever repay you?"

The Englishman shrugged. "Don't mention it."

"Well, the offer is there. If at any time there's anything we can do for you, make sure you let us know," Joe said. He nodded, adding finality to the offer and disallowing any argument.

Winking at Joe, Hugh assumed a businesslike manner and turned to Charley. "We have a herd of reindeer at Roddickton," he said in a serious tone, "and we're driving them to Millertown in central Newfoundland. Would you like to come along?"

The boy was about to accept, but his mother interrupted. "I think Charley is better here at home!" she said in an alarmed voice.

Hugh laughed. Of course he knew Charley couldn't go, but at least he had given the boy food for thought, something to fuel his imagination and take his mind off his discomfort.

Before leaving, Hugh and Mattie asked if there was anywhere in town they could buy two strong dogs. Mark reminded them that he and his father had lost their own team through the ice at Bide Arm earlier in the winter. "But I'll go around Englee with you," he volunteered, "and try to locate a couple of dogs for you."

Thanking Fanny and the rest of the family for the warm meal and their hospitality, Hugh Cole and Mattie Mitchell shook hands with Charley and wished him a speedy recovery. They smiled when they looked back at the sick young man. He was deep in thought, no doubt dreaming of countless adventures on the reindeer trail.

10

IN 1908, MARCH WAS called the long and hungry month. This year in particular brought with it extreme poverty, and it was a desperate time for people along the coast. On top of that, the weather was cold and stormy most of that month, with the wind blowing in a northwesterly direction. Englee was one of many towns affected. Around these small Newfoundland towns, most people stemmed from families that were related to each other from the sixth cousin down. Most called their elders either Uncle or Aunt. Families, which were large, usually worked together. When a husband or wife died, the surviving spouse would marry another partner as quickly as possible. Family allowance, old-age pension, and unemployment insurance were unknown in those days. Relief, known as "the dole," was difficult to obtain. The number one thing people looked for was work. Few people were put on salary, and money was uncommon.

During his stay at Englee, Hugh Cole and his companions bought supplies for their long journey. His diary records that, by Thursday, March 26, he was in the Lake Mitchell area and out of food; Englee had been desperately short on provisions. The same held true at Lock's Cove. It was ironic that Newfoundland, a colony of Great Britain, depended mostly on foreign aid, when Canada was so close and prosperous.

The month of March was a hectic one for Dr. Grenfell as well. He encountered many problems introducing his reindeer to the Great Northern Peninsula. Some of the herders had been brought in from Labrador, but most had been hired from St. Anthony. The Laplander families proved to be difficult as well: language barriers and adjusting to the climate and living conditions in St. Anthony greatly reduced the Europeans' efficiency. Also, the doctor couldn't spend as much time on this project as he would have liked. He was frequently called way to attend to medical needs elsewhere in Newfoundland.

There were no seals or fish. The wildlife and caribou supply had been depleted. By Monday, April 6, Fanny Hancock had decided that, in order to obtain food for her family, a move had to be made. The family despaired when she cooked the last remaining morsel. Now they found themselves in a tight spot, with absolutely nothing to eat. It was decided unanimously that they would send someone to Flower's Cove, on the northwestern side of the Great Northern Peninsula, to obtain food. Opposite Quebec on the Newfoundland side of the Strait of Belle Isle, Flower's Cove was a good source of fish and seals, and the people of Englee had used it before in times of need. Although only fifty-five miles from Englee, in those days Flower's Cove seemed like the other side of the world.

THE PRICE PAID FOR CHARLEY

However, Joe Hancock knew the way across. The weather was mild and fog rested atop the hills on the day he decided to go out. A few of the smaller brooks had melted, but the large rivers were still safe to travel.

The first of Joe's problems was getting enough food together to sustain him for the long trip. Fanny went to the storeroom where the family kept their flour barrels. The two large containers were empty, but she had an idea. She took a fork and ran it up and down the seams, gouging out enough flour to make a small cake of bread. The whole family pitched in and went out to the fishing stage. There they managed to find a piece of seal fat to add to his meagre lunch. Satisfied that he had all he needed, young Joe bid his family a fond farewell, carrying with him their hopes against starvation.

Friday, April 10 found Charley in pain as his leg flared up. The doctor's incision had almost healed over, but the small opening that remained near his knee had started to throb dully in the last few days. It was oozing pus constantly, and the ache that had developed kept him awake nights. Aunt Lizzie Gillard was summoned. She dressed the wound and advised Charley to keep his leg elevated. This eased the pain a little, and Charley was grateful to be able to fall asleep again.

When he awoke and lowered his leg in the evening, however, the blood started circulating and he swooned as his knee resumed its daily complaint. Fanny helped him lift his leg, and immediately the pain subsided. Giving Charley a worried look, she went to the kitchen to see if there was any food, anything at all, to give to her son. Her eyes widened as she remembered she had stored a piece of bread for just such an occasion. She toasted it the way Charley liked it and offered it to him.

Joe was gone, but Charley was now her main concern. She called Aunt Lizzie, and the midwife came over at once. She removed the dressing she had applied and gave the boy's knee a thorough examination. Shaking her head, the midwife turned to Fanny, confirming her fears. Charley's leg was getting worse.

Just before sunset the next day, Roy spotted someone walking out of the woods on the other side of Bide Arm, two miles away. He shielded his eyes against the dying sun with an upraised hand. It was Joe. He had returned at last from Flower's Cove. Roy, the oldest of the Hancock brothers, commanded the others to ready a komatik so they could meet Joe. In minutes they were off, anxious to learn what he had found. There was an excited yell when they neared their exhausted brother. He was carrying a large bag on his back, and a gallon can dangled from his hand.

When they reached him, Joe collapsed. The bag he was carrying had been lashed to his body with straps he had fashioned out of some thin line. The brothers saw that the straps had cut into him, deep enough to draw blood in some places. His glove had frozen to the heavy can. They cut him free in a matter of seconds. They rejoiced when they discovered that the hundred-pound bag Joe carried was filled with flour, and the can with molasses. He was brought to the house and put to bed, and Fanny found herself dividing her time between him and Charley. Aunt Lizzie came over to lend a hand, bandaging

THE PRICE PAID FOR CHARLEY

Roy's shoulders and examining him for any further injuries. Relieved, she found that the cuts were the worst of it and that bedrest was the best thing for him now.

Emmie came back from Roddickton on Good Friday, April 17. She had stayed there for a month while her husband cut logs for Dr. Grenfell's sawmill. Aunt Lizzie told her about Charley's deteriorating health, and she raced over to the Hancocks' home before she'd even gotten a chance to rest.

"Charley is in a very bad state," the young midwife said to Fanny after she gave the boy's leg a cursory glance. "He's even worse than when Dr. Grenfell operated on him. The infection is now in his knee. Aunt Fanny, do you know how this happened?"

Charley's mother could offer no reply, so Emmie pressed on. "Dr. Grenfell said to make sure the operation was draining at all times. Aunt Fanny, what went wrong?"

"Nothing," Fanny said despondently. "We put Charley's leg high on the pillows. It was the only way we could get him to sleep."

Emmie was furious. "Charley's whole leg is infected now," she accused. "There's nothing I can do for him! It's a case for the hospital now, for sure. From what I can see, Aunt Fanny, it has turned to TB."

Tuberculosis. Fanny felt like she was going to faint. "What do you mean, Emmie?" she asked in a voice that sounded far away.

Emmie sighed. "Aunt Fanny," she said calmly, "we've got to get Charley to St. Anthony. You should have taken him there a week ago, as soon as his leg started paining." She knew a bad storm was approaching on the wind, blowing southeast and carrying freezing rain with it, but they had no choice. Charley would have to be admitted to the hospital.

"I want a cup of tea, please, Aunt Fanny."

"Okay, Emmie."

The young midwife sat down. Fanny brought her a mug of weak tea, and she took two small sips.

"I know the tea isn't fit to drink," Fanny said apologetically, "but that's all we've got. "

"It's all right, Aunt Fanny. Now, here's what we'll do. If the weather is a bit co-operative tomorrow, we'll take Charley to St. Anthony. Start getting him ready, because he has to go, no questions asked."

"I'll get him ready for travel, but I'm not sure if he'll be able to make the trip."

"He has to make it," Emmie said firmly, standing as if to emphasize her point. "I'm going to have to talk with my husband, Esau. He might be able to get some men on the move. It's no use trying to get Dr. Grenfell to come here to operate on Charley again. Your son's best bet is the hospital." With that, she drained her tea and left to make her own preparations.

Fanny sat at the table for a long time and thought, as she had so many times lately, of the troubles she had lived through this winter. She buried her face in her hands and wept. After awhile, she looked at the bedroom door, listening for the sound of Charley's snoring. "In there is a prisoner," she murmured.

That thought got her moving. "Yes," she said. "We've

imprisoned him, and now he's slowly dying in captivity. And for what reason? Just why haven't we taken him to the hospital?" She glanced around the room frantically. "I can send my sons to walk alone through the forest and mountains, and yet I can't send my dying son to the hospital. Why, why, why?"

She dropped to her knees. "Dear God," she prayed, "help me. Please open up a way—some way—whereby we can get Charley to the hospital. I know, dear God, that we may have waited too long, but I know You can do anything if we put our trust in You."

Dr. Grenfell spent most of Good Friday visiting patients at his St. Anthony hospital. His willingness, determination, and drive were without equal, and he spent the day around the wards and his staff's living quarters, speaking with people wandering the grounds. He raised courage, boosted morale, and helped people to surmount pain and live better lives.

He had little connection to the outside world, only letters he received every two months. (There were no telephones or wireless in those days. Mail arrived by dog team, and there was always an exciting moment shared by all when the mailman brought in his mailbag.) He could have stayed in his hometown, the great city of London, England, and lived a comfortable and prosperous life, but this was not the desire of the distinguished gentleman with the broad shoulders and always-smiling face. He loved God and was willing to make sacrifices.

He was destined, but not for the hospital wards around London. The God who controls Man's destiny, but who gives him free will, had sent a young Wilfred Grenfell on a long journey, to be tossed in the mighty Atlantic Ocean, battered by wind and rain, strapped at night to the mast in a northeaster, clutching the tiller in a roiling sea. His destiny and destination, Newfoundland, had cried out to him those many years ago to come and give her a fighting chance, to breathe the life back into her. And now each time Dr. Grenfell's heart pumped, it beat a directive to his soul, to help the dying and suffering, to help the lost, to help the destitute and lonely.

As he made his way around the hospital grounds, his thoughts drifted far away, to a different place and time. In 1892, a girl had died in his care, the first of many, but this one had touched him in a profound way. This young woman had been with child, and the shame of it had kept her from revealing her sickness to those around her. Pride had won the day over the value of human life. She was never given a fighting chance.

This had become Dr. Grenfell's calling, to educate as well as nurture those in need. Life had a purpose, and it was up to him to show it to those who didn't know. His days with Captain Trezise aboard the *Albert* were long gone now, but the image of that frightened young woman never left him.

Even on Good Friday, when most people were idle, Dr. Grenfell's mission was clear. Help the suffering. Help the dying. Help everyone but yourself.

11

THE NORTHEAST WIND BLEW a gale, accompanied by wet, driving snow. Its rawness pierced the clothing of any on the Great Northern Peninsula who dared to venture outside, its howl singing a death knell to the foolhardy. No one on this part of the peninsula visited his neighbour today, nor were there any church services. It was too stormy. Some old-timers predicted that the storm would last for three days and that a big sea was guaranteed to heave.

In Englee, as in most other towns in Newfoundland, Good Friday was a sacred day, but there was little cause for celebration in the Hancock household. Charley cried continuously; his pain was unbearable. His voice had sunk to little more than a whisper, but loud enough to torment his family with his agony. He was feverish, perilously so; his lips cracked and his mouth was sore. His leg had swollen and had turned dark. Tuberculosis was ravaging the bone in his leg. All bones in the human body are interrelated, framing the human skeleton, and because of this Charley was racked with pain from head to toe.

He could not eat. Even if he could, there were few nutrients or vitamins to offer him. Charley just lay on his back, enduring the pain of a serious bone infection and a swiftly decaying thigh.

The Hancock family sat around Charley's bed, not knowing what to expect. Aunt Lizzie had told them not to move their patient, despite Aunt Emmie's insistence that they take poor Charley to the hospital in St. Anthony. To take him by komatik and attempt to haul him sixty miles overland, on a rough ice road, across brooks, or even on bare ground, would be suicidal. Dr. Grenfell would have to be called back to Englee.

In the afternoon the Methodist minister, Reverend C. B. Tiller, accompanied by some men who had stopped over because of the storm, came by the house to pray with Charley. The minister commented to Fanny that Charley seemed to be fading fast and that he did not expect the boy to last much longer. Nothing short of a miracle would save her son, he said. Fanny didn't like his remarks, and she told him so.

"How do you know," she asked, "that Charley won't last long? Your job, Reverend, is to bury the dead, but our job is to make sure you don't have to—or at least delay it. As for Charley, he's going to St. Anthony, even if I have to carry him there on my back!"

"I'm sorry, Aunt Fanny," replied Reverend Tiller. "I didn't mean to upset you. I'm sorry, my dear. I know you are going through a rough time.

"Yes, I am," she said indignantly, "but what I can't understand is why all these men around here aren't on their way to the hospital. If I were a man, I'd crawl on my hands and knees to St. Anthony. Can't someone see that?"

The minister started to reply, but Fanny turned away and walked to the woodbox, bending to load wood into the stove. Reverend Tiller motioned to the men who had accompanied him, and they left.

By Saturday morning the storm had eased somewhat. Light rain still blew, but the snow at least had abated. At daybreak two dog teams were made ready to go. The teams consisted of twenty-six dogs and accommodated four men, and each komatik was equipped with a coach box. Roy Hancock came out of his house and Peter Lane waved at him. Peter, who was in charge of the teams, knew the route between Englee and Hare Bay.

"Charley can't be moved, Peter," Roy said when he approached. "We'll have to go on ahead and bring the doctor back. Mother is frantic. She's been walking the floor all night."

"Then what are we waiting for, Roy? Let's go!" The plan was to relay the message to Dr. Grenfell and bring back some supplies, if possible. They assumed the doctor would travel on his own dog team.

The thirty-five-mile distance from Englee to Hare Bay took sixteen hours to traverse. They arrived at Joseph Ollerhead's log cabin at Main Brook late in the evening. Roy and Peter hit the ground running, opened the door, and called out to Joseph.

"We'll be staying all night if you've got room," Peter said.

"I've got room. Are you on your way to St. Anthony?"

"Yes," said Peter. "I want you to meet Roy Hancock. His brother is sick."

Joseph nodded to Roy. "Only two of you?"

"Yes," replied Peter. "We've got sixteen dogs in our team, and all are on a trawl trace. We'll have to get them tied somewhere. We had to leave two men in a cabin at Lane's Pond. A lot of the dogs got cut up; their paws were slashed to pieces."

"No problem," said Joseph. "Just go out there behind the cellar and tie them to the trees."

Peter nodded, and he and Roy left.

They released the dogs from their harnesses and secured each animal to a tree for the night, then returned to the house. Mrs. Ollerhead, who was used to entertaining visitors, had lunch ready for them. Her house was a stopping-off point for most who passed through. Sitting at the table, Joseph Ollerhead anxiously pumped them for information as they ate.

"Roy," he began, "you said that your brother is sick."

"Yes, he has a bad leg."

"Is that the fellow Dr. Grenfell operated on awhile back?"

Roy nodded.

"So, he's sick again?"

"Yes, only this time he's much worse."

"Well," Joseph said, "you sure picked a good time to go for a doctor."

Peter gestured toward the window. "I think 'tis the worst I've ever seen. We had to cut a trail about three miles. We couldn't get across the river, so we went all the way to the lake. There's water over that, too."

THE PRICE PAID FOR CHARLEY

"There's a lot of water," Joseph agreed. "We had a bad storm here yesterday. The ice in Hare Bay is breaking up, and I've got a feeling there's a big sea heaving. If that happens it won't be long before all the ice breaks up. If the wind comes off the bay in a few days, there'll be nothing but clear water."

"Maybe you're right," said Peter. "You'll have no problem going across to Goose Tickle Arm from here in the morning, but I wouldn't go across the bay. It can be tempting, but don't think it's not dangerous. What you should do is go in around the bay, and before you come to Boiling Brooks you should be able to cross to Hare Island. From there you could cross to the Fox Hole. You'll be able to see what's happening when you get there, but if the ice is cracked, make sure the wind is not off west or northwest."

"Yes, we will," Joseph said, grateful for the advice.

Roy and Peter pushed their empty plates away and Mrs. Ollerhead placed several cups of tea in front of them. Gradually the conversation shifted to Dr. Grenfell's reindeer herd.

"Boy, oh boy!" said Joseph. "Imagine! The other day, fifty of those animals came along by my door with these fellows, Hugh Cole and Mattie Mitchell. Does Dr. Grenfell know what he's doing, I wonder? My son, there's enough dogs down around Quirpon and Griquet to eat every one of those reindeer in one night!"

"Yes, I'd say there are," Peter said, grinning.

"They say that Dr. Grenfell has a fellow in from Labrador, though," Joseph amended, "one of those mountaineer Indians." He was referring to a Montagnais Indian by the name of Charley Broomfield. Dr. Grenfell had brought him in especially as a herdsman to care for the dog problem. The rest of the evening passed quickly, and it was obvious that Joseph Ollerhead would rather hunt the woodland caribou that roamed the barrens of the Great Northern Peninsula than go to the St. Anthony area to view Dr. Grenfell's reindeer.

Roy and Peter followed the shoreline around Hare Bay the next day, Easter Sunday. Their sixteen dogs were strung out on a single rope, each about four feet apart. Some of the animals had been cut badly and their paws had to be wrapped. The trip itself was rough, but they made progress despite the unfavourable conditions. They went to Dr. Grenfell's log cabin on Nanserie Island, almost halfway around Hare Bay. Examining the bay ice there, they decided it was suitable for crossing to Lock's Cove, and they set out at once, keeping toward the Boiling Brooks–Hare Island side. The ice seemed to be moving farther into the open ocean, borne along by the heaving sea. The dogs had no fear, however, and obeyed their masters.

At 11:00 a.m. they arrived at Lock's Cove and went directly to see George Reid, the gentleman Mattie Mitchell and Hugh Cole had met on their way to pick up the reindeer herd. As soon as Roy introduced himself, George's eyes widened in recognition. He vigorously shook hands with the young man and added that he was at his disposal.

"Just say the word," George said. "We know all about Charley. Hugh Cole almost went over the cliffs in a blizzard, going to St. Anthony to get the news to Dr. Grenfell. The doctor got to Charley in time and operated on him, I hear."

"Yes," Roy said, instantly taking a liking to the man, "but now he's very sick again." He hung his head. "He may even be dead by now, Mr. Reid."

George laid a reassuring hand on Roy's shoulder. "Keep your head above water, son," he said.

He gave the visitors some tea and bread from his personal stores, and the two ate quickly, apologizing for not being able to stay and chat with this kind gentleman. George said he understood, and he hurried them out the door himself.

It was a little better moving on the open country, with visibility being fairly clear. The dogs were beginning to weary before long, however, and the closer they got to St. Anthony, the more noticeable the limp in their gait became. Roy and Peter were determined to reach St.Anthony, regardless of the circumstances, so they pushed the dogs even harder.

They arrived on the outskirts of the town at 1:00 p.m., the road they were following taking them directly to Dr. Grenfell's hospital. Stopping at the front gate, they hitched their animals to the posts that were provided for precisely that reason. A group of teenagers, attracted by the excitement, approached. Peter Lane knew one of them, and he quickly relayed the reason they had come to St. Anthony. The word spread around the community that poor Charley was dying, and that the doctor was needed at Englee immediately.

That Easter Sunday dawned miserably in Englee, with rain and gusting wind. No snow was blowing but the sea was heaving, as Joseph Ollerhead had predicted. This was causing an ominous rumble amidst the heavy Arctic ice that had pushed to shore. Charley Hancock was no better. He cried and cried, fainted occasionally, and awakened only to resume his wailing.

Aunt Lizzie Gillard stopped by to see him, and declared that he would not survive another day. He could not be moved, as this would only increase his discomfort. The men around Englee knew that Dr. Grenfell could not possibly reach them in time, but each one held his peace around Aunt Fanny.

The Hancock family sat around wearing blank expressions, all hope gone of Charley ever recovering. Some wondered where he would be buried. Others wondered if Roy would ever see his brother alive again.

Dr. Grenfell walked toward the hospital after the Easter Sunday morning church service. He was excited, having just given a rousing speech to the congregation. He walked with a spring in his step and sang as he walked.

"Dr. Grenfell! Dr. Grenfell!" a teenager called loudly as he ran toward the doctor.

"Yes, son. What is it?" The boy was out of breath, and the doctor noticed a look of fear on his face.

"A large dog team has just arrived at the hospital from Englee. They need you to go with them. They say that Charley is dying, Doctor! They need you immediately."

"Okay," the doctor said, quickening his pace.

Dr. Grenfell was dressed in a long sealskin coat and a pair of skin-boots. Underneath he wore a heavy tweed winter suit.

THE PRICE PAID FOR CHARLEY

He looked more distinguished now than he had in Roddickton, and Roy did a double take when the doctor approached.

"Dr. Grenfell," he managed, "Charley is sick again."

"How sick, Roy? It is Roy, isn't it?"

"Yes, Doctor. He's very sick—he could be dead by now."

Dr. Grenfell put his hands on his hips. "Did they follow my instructions?" he asked, a touch of doubt creeping into his voice.

"Yes, I think so, Doctor."

"Where is he having the pain—"

Interrupting himself, he shook his head and turned to a nurse standing nearby. "Will you get me ready for an emergency trip to Englee? Prepare the instruments for an amputation. Make sure the kit has all the necessary instruments, dressings, and drugs. Also, call Reuben Simms and tell him that I want eight of my best dogs, and I want the komatik with the copper shoes." Used in mild weather, the copper would sometimes prevent snow from sticking to the vehicle. "I'll be going alone this time. Pack enough food for two nights."

"Yes, Doctor," the nurse said and hurried off.

He turned to Roy. "Where is he having the pain?" he repeated.

"The pain, Doctor, seems to be all over him. His leg has turned black and his knee is swollen, very large."

Dr. Grenfell nodded. "Has he a fever?"

"Yes, and sometimes his teeth rattle. It seems like he's freezing."

"Does he have a stiff jaw?" the doctor asked, thinking that

Charley might have tetanus. More than likely it was the fever running through his body, he thought.

"I'm not sure, Doctor. Most of the time Aunt Lizzie is with him by herself, and Charley can't even talk because of the pain."

"It's serious enough, Roy, but I think that he can live for a while yet." The doctor paused. "There's only one remedy that I can see, and that is to amputate the leg. I'd say he has TB in his knee by now. Did they keep the operation open?"

"No," said Roy. "I overheard Emmie and Aunt Lizzie in an argument over the same thing. Emmie was gone for a month to Roddickton."

"Well, well," said the doctor. He thought of the young girl who had been with child back in 1892, and of the family she feared would disown her because of it. It seemed that what was in the best interest of the patient was often in conflict to that of his or her family. "Roy, we can leave as soon as you have a cup of tea. I'll go on ahead, and we'll meet up at Lock's Cove."

"Okay, Doctor," Roy said, surprised tears coming to his eyes. There might be a chance for Charley yet.

12

THE ENGLISH DOCTOR OFTEN said that if a person says he is a Christian and does not love animals, then he does not love God. If a person poaches animals, he is a thief, because poaching is stealing. He insisted that a person should love dogs in particular. Dr. Grenfell had an outstanding dog team. Wherever he went with his team, his dogs would be the topic of conversation for days. In order to drive a dog team, one must know the dogs and their individual strengths. The animals must be disciplined to obey commands to the letter. A master who shows his dog team little or no discipline is a master who displays no love, the doctor said. He showed his team much discipline, and his dogs responded with love in kind.

Each dog team has a lead dog. A leader is usually broken in for its duty as soon as it matures from a pup. Many stories have been told about Dr. Grenfell's leader, Brin. This dog had a brownish colour resembling burlap (or brin) bags in which potatoes were packed for shipment. Thus, the name had stuck. A clever and faithful dog, Brin could take the English doctor over the barrens of the White Hills in blizzards with zero visibility.

Next to Brin was Doc. This dog was extremely powerful, a large animal with nearly limitless endurance. Doc was quiet and resembled a Labrador retriever in appearance. He could be driven in the leader's place, but was used mostly for power.

The third dog was Moody, named after the evangelist Dwight L. Moody. As a young man Dr. Grenfell attended university in London, England. One night he had walked into a revival meeting in a huge downtown hall. Inspirational singing filled the place. Then the evangelist Moody stepped to the podium, a large man full of fire. When he opened his Bible and started preaching, it seemed the power in his words caused the building to shake. A moving experience for Dr. Grenfell, it branded him for the remainder of his life. That night he had been converted. He became a Methodist and would never change his church affiliation. The dog with the holy man's namesake was a kind animal, with a long, heavy coat and big, powerful legs. Although large, Moody was a fast runner.

Next in line was Watch. He was a young animal with childlike eyes that appeared to be full of tears all the time. Watch had a rich golden setter coat that was quite beautiful to all who beheld it. A willing worker, he was an agile runner, too. Spy, a powerful black-and-white dog, could run all day in almost any weather and still be anxious for a dash afterwards. Dr. Grenfell thought a lot of Spy.

Sue was a huge Eskimo dog. In truth the doctor was out-

THE PRICE PAID FOR CHARLEY

right scared of this one. A large, black, wolflike animal, Sue barked constantly, introducing everyone within earshot to her wild ancestry. At night the dog would turn wild and needed to be isolated from her teammates.

Jerry, another female dog, was maroon in colour and bore a comical resemblance to a cat. Extremely quick, she could jump and play at any time. An affectionate animal, Jerry was always in good humour, and a fast runner besides.

Jack, the retriever, was jet-black. A gentle dog, he was Dr. Grenfell's "hinor," whose job was to run next to the sled. He looked straight ahead all the time and pulled with his nose to the ground. A magnificent dog with short, black hair, Jack loved being put in harness.

Dr. Grenfell had not only been a medical student at Oxford University, but also an athlete who employed his skills at the game of football. He was a hard worker, and this kept him in excellent physical shape. While at university he had been issued a football uniform. Upon finishing his medical degree, he had packed his uniform and stored it, not setting eyes on it again until well after arriving in Newfoundland. On this day, while packing his things for the trip, he decided to wear part of his football gear. He donned the uniform and was pleased to see that it still fit. Reminiscing about his college days, he threw in extra clothes and a pair of sealskin boots for the journey, his rifle, compass, oilskins, axe, and snowshoes. His packing completed, he took the clothes bag to his office, where a nurse relieved him of it and carried it outside.

The word was passed that Reuben Simms was bringing Dr.

Grenfell's team to the front of the hospital. A group of people, mostly children, had gathered to watch the proceedings. Dr. Grenfell was, besides many other things, a showman. He loved attention, and wherever he went he attracted lots of it. All who were in any way associated with Dr. Grenfell considered him an extraordinary person. His was a household name on the Great Northern Peninsula, in Labrador, and along the Quebec North Shore.

Roy Hancock and Peter Lane had finished their meal and prepared their own dogs to move. A man had brought them two large boxes of supplies and rough foodstuffs. The two men from Englee secured their belongings, and Peter had a word with Dr. Grenfell. The doctor agreed that he would go ahead, but would wait for Roy and Peter at Lock's Cove before crossing Hare Bay.

"You're sure, Dr. Grenfell," asked his driver, Reuben, "that you don't want me to go with you?"

"Yes," answered the doctor. "I'll be all right. You have the day with your family."

Reuben thanked him and wished him a safe journey.

Patients watched through the hospital windows as Dr. Grenfell stepped to the front of his komatik. The commotion of the barking dogs, the chattering people, the constant bustle of animal and man, lent an air of excitement to the onlookers. Their doctor was about to move out of St. Anthony using the fastest mode of transportation on the Great Northern Peninsula—the gallant dog team.

Just as the wind picked up speed from the northeast, the

signal was given. Dr. Grenfell was released from the hitching rail. He took off at breakneck speed, leaving the sound of the cheering crowd behind. The team made a mad dash for the White Hills and the open barrens, all of his dogs pumping their legs wildly.

He stopped two miles out, near the camp headquarters of his reindeer herd. He waited for the Englee team to catch up to his superior dogs. When they finally came into sight, he made a slight change in plans and said he wanted to stay overnight at Lock's Cove, due to the lateness of the day and some unfavourable weather he saw looming on the horizon. Roy started to protest, but Peter intervened.

"Okay, Doctor," Peter said.

Dr. Grenfell nodded and moved on.

"What in the world is he stopping for?" asked a surprised Roy.

"I don't know," Peter said and shrugged. "We could go around Hare Bay before dark. I think the wind is going to be off western."

Roy was fuming by the time they arrived at Lock's Cove. He knew that Dr. Grenfell would stick to his word and stay the night. Peter worked to calm his friend, though, explaining that he would be doing Charley no good by angering the only man who could help him. Throwing up his hands in disgust, Roy went to the home of Nathaniel Dawe with Peter in tow. Nat, one of the pioneers of Lock's Cove, had a reputation for making quality items from iron, and he was also famous for his hospitality.

Nat welcomed the travellers and told them that Dr. Grenfell had arrived a half-hour earlier and had announced an evening service at the school chapel.

"Mr. Dawe," Roy complained, "I've got a sick brother—fifteen years old—back home. He was dying yesterday when we left, and I can't understand why Dr. Grenfell is staying here tonight. We should go on to Main Brook at least and stay the night at Joseph Ollerhead's. We've only been travelling for two hours!"

Nat didn't comment, but he was sympathetic.

"Mr. Dawe," Roy continued, "do you know why Dr. Grenfell won't go any farther this evening?"

"Well, Roy," Nat said, "when Dr. Grenfell arrived here just now, I got quite a shock. Reuben Simms, his driver, always travels with him, but the doctor came alone."

"That's no excuse," Roy shot back. "I could go with him and drive his dogs."

"My son, listen! If you ever stepped aboard Dr. Grenfell's komatik, his dogs would eat you alive. By rights I'd say that Dr. Grenfell is afraid and doesn't want to be caught out with them after dark."

"So, Charley has to suffer longer, or maybe even die," Roy said bitterly, "just because Dr. Grenfell is afraid of his dogs."

"Roy," Peter interjected, "whatever it is or whatever it isn't, we've got to put up with it. Take it easy."

Roy said no more. He walked outside and secured his dogs for the night. When he left St. Anthony, he had possessed renewed energy, purpose, and the reborn hope that the

THE PRICE PAID FOR CHARLEY

youngest of the Hancock boys would survive his worst trial yet. And now this!

But what Roy didn't know was that it would take the English doctor two more days to reach his brother's bedside.

Fanny had given up hope that Dr. Grenfell would arrive before Charley died. She had not eaten all day. It seemed to her that she was cursed never to have just one thing to worry about at a time. Her son Joe had braved the elements to bring back enough food to keep them going for a while, but he was in terrible shape when he returned. Then there was Roy. There was no telling where he was, or even if he had managed to reach St. Anthony.

"Why haven't they come back?" she asked aloud.

Charley's leg was swollen, his hip turned black. His pain was so intense he had to be held down. People were sitting at his bedside all the time. He would open his eyes for a few moments and groan pitifully, saliva running from the corners of his mouth. "Mother! Mother! Please help me! I can't stand the pain!" he would call, but there was no relief for him.

The weather was poor, and Fanny knew that some of the brooks had melted. She hoped Roy hadn't dared go on the ice at Hare Bay. The men in Englee were talking about the heavy sea breaking up the ice in Canada Bay and Bide Arm. They said they could expect the same in Hare Bay.

Around 7:00 p.m. Zacharias Canning, a young man in his late teens, and brother to Emmie Fillier, dropped by the Hancock house. He greeted Fanny and asked to see her sick son. She showed him to the patient's room, and he entered, sitting near the younger boy.

"How are you, Charley?" he asked.

"I'm still sick."

"You'll be better again." His reassurance was met with silence. "Charley, 'tis going to clear away, and the wind is going off western. Early tomorrow morning we're going to have fine weather." This young man, known locally as "Sack," was for years regarded as the weather forecaster in the Roddickton–Englee area.

Fanny, who stood nearby, caught his prediction. "What was that, Sack?" she queried.

"'Tis going to clear away overnight, Aunt Fanny."

"So what?" she retorted hotly. "That won't help!"

Sack looked at her for a long moment. "Aunt Fanny," he said, "do you know what I'd do if I were you?"

Fanny folded her arms but did not answer.

"I'd get a couple of boats ready, and the minute the ice slackened, I'd put Charley aboard and take him to St. Anthony."

Fanny jumped. "Sack," she said sharply, "do you know what you're talking about?"

The young man nodded.

"I mean about the weather. How do you know what the weather is going to be like tomorrow, Sack?"

"Well," he explained, "this is Sunday, the nineteenth of April. We haven't seen the sun for ten days. Last month it crossed the line on good weather, and tomorrow will be a

THE PRICE PAID FOR CHARLEY

month. We've had easterly winds now for six days, and the old people used to say that a southwester is always in debt to a northwester. So, there'll be a change tonight."

Fanny blinked. She said, "Sack, get your sister Emmie for me, okay? Tell her that I want her right away. And tell Mark to get his big carcass here as fast as he can"

"Okay, Aunt Fanny," said Sack, and he went away with a frightened look on his face.

13

ALL CHURCH SERVICES IN Lock's Cove were held in the small school building. A screen was pulled across the back in such cases, such as tonight. Dr. Grenfell began in a voice clear and crisp.

"I would like to wish all of you a happy Easter. We are gathered here this evening to worship God. As you all know, the stone has been rolled away, and we have hope." He led two hymns and followed with a rousing sermon. It was a moving experience for the people of Lock's Cove to have the famed English doctor speak to them on this Easter Sunday evening. After the meeting he went to George Reid's home and sent a message to Roy and Peter, telling them to continue their journey in the morning but to wait for him at his line camp near Nanserie Island. He would follow as soon as his dogs were ready for travel.

Roy and Peter asked the messenger to let Dr. Grenfell know that they would be leaving early and that they would wait for him around Hare Bay. Nat Dawe told the two not to go near the ice.

THE PRICE PAID FOR CHARLEY

"You can hear it breaking up with the sea heaving," Nat said. "By tomorrow morning there'll only be slob ice left, and it looks like we're going to have the wind off northwest."

"We won't be going near the ice, sir," said Roy.

"Take the line that's best, and go in over the hill."

"Yes, we will," Peter promised. "I've gone there before. I know where to go."

"I guess that's the way Dr. Grenfell will be going, so you'd better get a move on," said Nat. "He has a pretty smart team, all eight of them."

Peter grinned. "Don't worry, Mr. Dawe. We'll go around the bay as quickly as Dr. Grenfell. Our team can haul three teams like his any day."

"I'd say you're right," Nat laughed. Roy joined in, and soon all three were laughing.

Hours before daybreak on Monday, April 20, Allan Hancock walked to the ocean. The sea roared in his ears. The very air he breathed was dense and tinged with salty spray. It seemed like he could even smell the kelp from the ocean and the debris littering the shoreline. Gazing at the horizon in the dim morning light, he noticed the clouds moving off.

This is a sign of the wind—west or northwest. It's off, all right, he thought. *I think I should get word to Mark.*

He checked his boat, a twenty-two-foot trap boat used for hauling cod traps. It was a stable vessel that had been built wide. Last night a group of men had put a small house on board, big enough to hold Charley Hancock. There was even room for the midwife, Emmie Fillier, to sit near him. Everyone in Englee knew it would have to be this way: Charley would have to be taken to the hospital in St. Anthony by boat, or he would die. Fanny and the midwives readied Charley for the strenuous trip, while the people kept their fears to themselves that he would die en route.

Mark checked the weather. The wind was off, and the ice was already moving out from Canada Bay, which had an indraft of twenty miles. The town of Englee is built around three islands, the largest of which is Englee Island. The second is French Island and the third Barred Island, the latter of which protects the harbour of Englee from the great swells that roll in from the ocean.

By the time Charley reached the boat, daylight had arrived. The patient, although wrapped warmly, was suffering every minute. He loved boats, though, and wasn't scared when told he was going aboard.

"We're going to have a beautiful day, Aunt Fanny," said one of the men as the group moved toward the shore. Dim lights glowed in the houses, and many people stood in their doorways, offering encouragement.

Charley was placed on board the skiff and made comfortable in the small house. Six of Englee's strongest men, including the woodcutters Aaron Reid and Mark Hancock, boarded and took their place as rowers. Emmie placed six hot water bottles around Charley and sat by his side. A strange look came over the young man's face then. He was listening to something. Then she heard it, too.

THE PRICE PAID FOR CHARLEY

"God be with you till we meet again, by His counsel's guide, uphold you, with His sheep securely fold you, God be with you till we meet again . . ."

The people who had gathered on the shores of Englee to see Charley off were singing.

Dr. Grenfell ate a breakfast of cooked rolled oats and toast. It was light out, not yet six o'clock. He had been awake most of the night, going over in his mind several problems that had arisen as of late. He had thought much about his newest venture, the reindeer herd. It was a gamble, but the project's success was guaranteed if the government co-operated. He knew the locals were enthusiastic, but . . .

"The two men from Englee left very early, Doctor," said George Reid, interrupting his thoughts.

"Do you know what time they went, George?"

"One hour before daylight. Almost every dog in the town was barking."

The doctor raised an eyebrow. "I never heard a sound. Which way did they go?"

"They went over the ridge, on your cut line around the bottom of the bay."

"What do you think the going is like on that trail?"

"I'd say not very good this morning," George said. "It froze a bit last night and the wind is off west. It looks like we're going to have a pretty good day. All the ice in the bay is broken up, too, and now it's all just mush. I'd say there's not an ice pan big enough for a harp seal to crawl up on now!"

"What's the going like along the shore, George?"

"I'd say 'tis not bad, but it could be rough. Why?"

"Maybe the trail in the woods has a lot of stumps or sticks on it," Dr. Grenfell said. "And me, with all my dogs on single traces . . . I could have a real problem. It's all right for those two fellows from Englee, because they have their dogs on a single line. "

"Maybe you're right. But whatever you do," George warned, "if you go along the shoreline, don't go on the ice or even near it."

"Oh, no, I won't go handy to that," Dr. Grenfell promised. "Would you get my dogs harnessed for me, please? I'm going to put on my football uniform again and go out on the field to represent old Oxford."

George laughed.

Mrs. Reid thought Dr. Grenfell's attire was extremely funny. She had never seen anything like it. Soon he was dressed and ready to go and his dogs were put to tackle. The signal was given, and he, in full regalia, was on the move again.

The English doctor moved swiftly along the shoreline near the edge of the trees. He stopped a couple of times to watch the sea, noticing the waves rippling beneath the ice. He peered into the miles-long bay.

If I cross here, he thought, *I could shorten my trip by at least twenty miles.*

The biggest problem he saw was getting onto the ice itself. The sea near the shoreline was a puzzle. George Reid's warning still rang in his ears, but the doctor was feeling guilty that he had waited at Lock's Cove when he knew that time was of the essence. His dogs had unnerved him, to the point where he didn't want to be alone with them after dark, but the guilt remained. Nudging his team, he continued along the shoreline. He came to a small cove sheltered from the ocean and stopped for a closer look.

"Yes," he said, "I can get onto the ice here."

He called to the leader, Brin. "Hold in!" The command signalled a left turn. The dog turned obediently and dashed for the ice, dragging his fellows behind. In less than ten seconds, Dr. Grenfell and his team were on solid ice. As they moved farther out, the swell increased. The doctor stopped the komatik and evaluated his situation. What he was standing on turned out to be slob ice, the loose, rolling type. It was packed tight, maybe four to six feet thick, but now that he was at sea level, the rolling swell was more apparent.

"I'd better get off," he said in a low voice.

He issued the command to keep off the ice, to make a right turn. Again his dogs obeyed without hesitation. He repeated the command until the entire team headed back to the shoreline, where they had first climbed onto the ice. Once he reached the shore, he looked out on the bay.

"I don't know, Uncle George," he said reflectively. "Maybe you're right, maybe you're wrong." He shrugged, deciding to continue along the shoreline.

He travelled another two miles. The going was tedious as he dragged the new komatik across gravel and rocks where the snow had melted. The sled took a heavy beating and the dog traces fared no better as they became tangled in the ice in places. The land started levelling, until he reached Fox Hole and its shelter from the sea. At Fox Hole people cut grass for their sheep and goats, and a few fed a cow or two. A well-forested area, its rivers teemed with salmon and trout during summer. The doctor pulled in to inspect the underside of his sled and shook his head when he saw the damage. His mind was made up. He would cross Hare Bay.

"Hold in, Brin! Hold in!" he shouted after mounting the sled again.

The leader abruptly jumped to the left. The other dogs followed, and within seconds Dr. Grenfell was on the ice once again. The swell was not as great here, so he decided to cross the three miles to Hare Island, thereby shortening his trip by six miles or so. George Reid's warning voice came to him again, but this time the doctor put it out of his mind. He tapped the komatik box with his whip's handle, calling to his dogs, "Move! Move! Move!"

The wind was a gale piercing from the northwest as the dogs raced and skimmed over the ice. Hare Island seemed to lunge toward the doctor. In the space of a few minutes, he neared the western point, but, to his surprise, he couldn't get ashore. A shoal near the point had made the sea treacherous between ice and land. He stopped the dogs before they got too close. "Shall I go back?" he questioned, glancing back at Fox Hole. "Or, shall I go farther in?" He looked at the bay. "I'll

THE PRICE PAID FOR CHARLEY

move along the shoreline," he decided. "I should be able to get back ashore up there."

As he ordered his dogs to move in a westerly direction, he noticed that the wind had picked up, blowing directly from the shore.

14

ROY AND PETER MOVED expertly around Hare Bay while the wind continued in a northwesterly direction. Theirs was a rough ride, but they had avoided crossing the ice so far. Looking across now, they questioned the wisdom of taking the long way to Englee.

"I'd say," Roy commented, "that Dr. Grenfell has gone across the bay to Brent Islands."

"Maybe you're right," said Peter. "At least he won't take the beating we just did."

They pressed on along the trail until they reached Boiling Brooks.

Peter grunted. "If this keeps up, there won't be a piece of ice left in Hare Bay by noon."

"I'd say so, too," Roy responded.

Soon they arrived at Dr. Grenfell's line camp and dismounted for a rest. An hour passed with no sign of the doctor, so after they had a mug-up, Peter and Roy decided to move on. If he had been on the trail, Dr. Grenfell would have caught up with them long before they reached the cabin. They concluded that the doctor must have crossed the ice to Brent Islands and gone on to Main Brook, where he would no doubt be waiting for them.

George Reid's boys accompanied Nat Dawe and his three sons to where they had buried their seal pelts, and just in time—the sea had started carrying away the valuable skins. They began the laborious work of hauling them to higher ground.

"If the wind keeps up," said Levi Dawe, noticing the ice near the shore was smooth and broken into smaller pieces, "the ice will go out of the bay pretty quick. We might be able to go out sealing in a couple of days." The others murmured in agreement.

"What do you think Dr. Grenfell will do, Uncle Nat?" asked one of George Reid's sons when the group broke for lunch.

Nat shrugged. "There's no way to predict what he'll do. He's a gambler, and gamblers take risks. However, crossing Hare Bay to Brent Islands is an awful risk."

"You never know," said Levi.

"No," said Nat, "I don't think Dr. Grenfell is that stupid."

"I'd sure like to have his team of dogs," the Reid boy said.

"Those dogs are capable of eating a man," Levi laughed. "That young Hancock fellow, Roy, was a woolly man last night when he got word that Dr. Grenfell wasn't going any farther. He wanted to know why, and if it wasn't for that fellow with him, I'd say the doctor would have heard something."

They gulped the last mouthfuls of lunch and returned to the task at hand in silence.

In the days of oar and sail, a sailor's wits were always put to the test.

A shoal called Island Cove Rocks is located four miles from Englee and near Conche, resting offshore about two hundred yards. When a heavy sea rolls in, it is dangerous to sail a boat between the shoreline and these breaking shoals, and if a northwest wind is blowing, one would even be hard pressed to go outside these shoals. On this day the sea roared thunderously as it slammed against the granite cliffs that lined the mighty Atlantic Ocean along the Great Northern Peninsula. The ice crept off the shoreline as the small boat's six oars sliced through the water like a knife. Allan Hancock studied the heavy seas as they moved their small boat into the white froth between the shoals and the shoreline. He focused on the undertow, the reversal of water into mighty swirling pools after it is thrown against the cliffs. The sea that rolled in was voluminous. After the third wave settled, the men strained against their oars and the boat shot ahead to the narrow gap between land and shoal.

Immediately the skiff began struggling in the undertow. The swirling surf underneath gripped the craft, like some massive beast holding a jittery, terrifed animal in its jaws before devouring it.

"Pull! Pull!" Allan roared above the sea.

The small boat fought courageously, like a young David

THE PRICE PAID FOR CHARLEY

defying a towering Goliath, propelled through the stubborn current as if by a hundred invisible horses.

A huge wave swamped the boat, throwing it near the cliffs.

"Stay to the oars, men!" Allan cried. "Don't lose control!"

The boat crested an enormous wave and the crew cast their eyes to the side, ever mindful that the shoreline and granite cliffs were less than fifty feet away.

"Head her off slightly, and pull hard!"

The boat was caught in a whirlpool. The six crewmen lost control momentarily as the little craft went into a spin.

"Hold her firm, men! Put her quarter on!"

A ten-foot wave loomed over the skiff. It ducked and shoved them toward the rocky crags and certain death.

"Push her back into the wave!" Allan commanded.

Reversing their strokes, the oarsmen stopped the forward motion of the boat. Another wave broke over them, and the craft was almost swamped again.

"Pull, men, pull!"

The crew struggled. They grunted with the exertion as they gave the oars everything they had. At last the boat pulled free and inched out of the whirlpool, clearing the shoreline.

Dr. Grenfell moved at a brisk pace along the soft, mushy ice. For quite some time now he had been aware that the texture of the smooth surface had changed subtly. Brin, his leader, looked back at him every few steps, as if sensing danger.

"Hold in!" the doctor called.

The team turned.

"Steady!" he ordered, meaning straight ahead.

Earlier, the pressure of the wind when it blew southeast had pounded the ice to a pulp. The mass had floated to the surface, leaving it covered with a thin layer of sticky slob that was full of chunks not much thicker than snow. Now the ice moved offshore with the strong northeast wind. If he had had any experience with such conditions, Dr. Grenfell would have kept farther toward the centre of Hare Bay and made a run for Brent or Long Islands. Instead, he called for his dog team to keep off. He planned to get ashore at the entrance to Seal Bay.

Suddenly a long expanse of water opened directly in front of Brin.

"Hold in!" the doctor screamed. "Hold in!"

The dogs dashed to the left, moving offshore. Dr. Grenfell's heart sank as their paws dipped into the slob and redirected them toward Nanserie Island. The animals' quick reflexes had prevented a worse fate, but the doctor began to feel a slow, creeping worry.

At noon Roy and Peter arrived at Joseph Ollerhead's cabin in Main Brook. Joseph was in the woods, but Mrs. Ollerhead told them he would be back shortly, so they sat down to eat.

Being ever talkative, Mrs. Ollerhead asked the visitors about the hard times they'd had along the coast. "St. Anthony," she said, "is the only place now that looks prosperous. I think that we should all move there to live and stop pretending that we're Indians." Peter agreed with her and joked that she should be running the country.

THE PRICE PAID FOR CHARLEY

At one-thirty Joseph arrived with a dead beaver and a packsack full of partridge. He plunked the bag down on a chair, seemingly unconcerned that his guests now knew of his poaching activities.

"You fellows made it back okay."

"Yes, we did," said Roy.

"Where's Dr. Grenfell?"

"We don't know."

"You don't know?" Joseph asked, puzzled.

Roy said the doctor had lagged behind. He added in an irritated tone of voice that Dr. Grenfell had felt it necessary to waste a night at Lock's Cove on account of his dogs.

"Well, boys," Joseph said, looking back and forth from Roy to Peter, "I've got no reason to call you liars, but that's a lot to swallow. Reuben Simms would never let Dr. Grenfell take that team of dogs and attempt to go to Englee alone, not unless he's planning to do away with him."

"He has the dog team himself," Roy said.

Joseph shook his head. "Listen, Dr. Grenfell could be halfway around Hare Bay with his neck broken."

"Joe," Mrs. Ollerhead argued, "it's Dr. Grenfell."

"We don't know if anyone from Lock's Cove came with him this morning," said Roy. "I bet you Uncle George Reid didn't let *Dr. Grenfell* leave Lock's Cove alone this morning!"

Joseph and his wife exchanged a curious glance when Roy emphasized the doctor's name, his voice dripping with sarcasm.

"But why isn't he here?" Joseph inquired. "That's a job to know." He was beginning to feel a little uneasy.

"We know that," said Roy, "but we were thinking that he attempted to cross the bay on the ice."

"Not a chance. I'd say that's one thing the crowd in Lock's Cove made sure of. Dr. Grenfell didn't cross that icy bay this morning."

Roy grunted. "They told us not to go near it and we took their advice. Maybe Dr. Grenfell wouldn't listen."

"Listen, boys. No man with a grain of sense would go handy to the ballicatter," Joseph argued, referring to the ice that formed along the shoreline by the rising and falling of the tide. "Don't even worry about Dr. Grenfell coming into Main Brook across the ice from Lock's Cove. If he was foolish enough to go on the ice, he's a goner."

"What can we do?" Peter asked anxiously.

"Do nothing," replied Joseph.

"We can't sit here all evening," said Roy, tapping his fingers on the table impatiently.

"The dogs are in bad shape. They're all cut to pieces," said Peter. "Let's go back to the cabin. There's not much else we can do."

"You're right," said Joseph. "Do you know what I'd do if I were you?"

The two men looked at him.

"I'd go on to Lane's Pond, where you left your two buddies before. When Dr. Grenfell arrives here, I'll tell him where you are."

"Maybe that's the proper thing to do, Peter," Roy said, turning to his companion. "We might have a lot of work to do on the trail between here and Lane's Pond."

THE PRICE PAID FOR CHARLEY

Joseph piped in. "Listen, before you go, I'm going to give you that beaver carcass and some partridge. We've got plenty of fresh for the spring." He motioned to the packsack he'd brought in.

"Well, thanks!" said Roy. "The boys at the camp will be pleased. "

Joseph went out to his shed and returned with a brin bag filled with fresh meat, including eighteen partridge. Peter and Roy loaded the bag into their komatik box, bidding the kindly Ollerheads goodbye before heading along the river toward Englee.

15

Dr. Grenfell's mind raced. He flashed a glance toward the shoreline, but he dared not go that way. If he went farther out on the ice, he would put himself in even greater danger. He had no experience with ice conditions and the seemingly unpredictable way the wind and tide interacted, so he headed straight for Nanserie Island. The closer he got, the softer the ice beneath his komatik became.

"I can't go on this island," he said in a conversational tone to his dogs. "I could be here for months and starve to death. I don't have any supplies. Hold in!"

Brin shot a glance at his master. Dr. Grenfell pointed him left and called again. They had almost reached the small island, but the lead dog obeyed his master without question, moving away from the supposed safety of the shore. The doctor spotted another location, a long point reaching into the bay. With a word, he headed his team there. Upon closer inspection he saw that a few large ice pans had been sheltered there from the force of the sea and remained intact. This looked promising.

THE PRICE PAID FOR CHARLEY

Without warning, Brin slipped through the slob ice. The leader regained his footing, but the doctor noted uneasily how the komatik began to settle as it moved. He knew he was headed into the water. The komatik slipped deeper and became harder to pull, the going made more desperate by the rolling swell. One moment the struggle was uphill, the next, downhill. The dogs weaved as they hauled on the steadily increasing weight of the sled.

Suddenly Brin went through again, this time sinking to his neck. Then two, four, eight of them were in the sticky slob. The komatik came to an abrupt stop.

Dr. Grenfell sat still for a moment. He looked at the shoreline, which was at least three hundred yards away. The severity of his predicament sobered him; he knew that he would have to enter the water himself. The entire ice surface moved as he looked around for a platform that could hold his weight. Thirty feet away he spied a piece of ice about twelve feet in diameter. "I must reach it," he said. This meant, of course, that he would have to push his way through the water.

The dogs whined and moaned, turning pitifully toward their master. Anchored to the komatik by their traces, they stood a good chance of perishing if the sled went through.

"What can I do?" Dr. Grenfell cried as he looked helplessly at his floundering dogs.

He thought of his knife, which boasted a six-inch blade, attached to his belt. Tearing off his skin gloves, he moved gingerly to the nose of the komatik. He reached for the bridle, a piece of rope attached to each side of the runners with a loop in the centre, serving as the centre of pull for the komatik. With a powerful stroke, he severed all eight traces at once, and each dog was released from the sled.

"I can't swim with this heavy coat on," he declared after a moment's consideration.

Quickly he removed it and plunged into the water. This man, this Dr. Grenfell, the man with the dream of helping the suffering, easing pain, taking in the orphan, healing broken hearts, the man with the hope of building hospitals, nursing stations, co-ops, and factories, raising herds of reindeer, angora sheep, cows, pigs, chickens, this man who put his trust in the God of Heaven, risked everything at that moment to meet the needs of a crippled fifteen-year-old patient, by jumping into the chilly ocean, not knowing if he would resurface. He sank into the salty ocean. Although a good swimmer, he found it difficult to tread water. He forced his arms forward and kicked furiously before forcing his head through the slob to resurface. Gulping air, he pulled his arms through the slob and rested them on the ice in front of him. He looked back at his dogs and komatik, then at the ice pan he intended to reach. The slob stuck to his body, preventing him from swimming any farther. The football suit he wore was soaked through like a mop in a bucket of oil.

To his horror, Dr. Grenfell saw the dogs struggling to reach him. At Roddickton he had heard the story of Skipper Jim Hancock's drowning at Bide Arm. The poor man's dogs, climbing upon him after he fell in the water, had kept him under until he had drowned. Young Mark Hancock had watched it all

THE PRICE PAID FOR CHARLEY

unfold, from beginning to end. The doctor called for his dogs to stop. To his amazement most of them obeyed. Still, some tried unsuccessfully to get on the komatik. He looked back at the pan of ice and searched for a way to get across.

He had an idea.

"Here, Brin!" he called. "Come here!"

The lead dog wrestled its way through the water to its master. Clutching the trace, the doctor ordered Brin to swim to the pan. The faithful dog started swimming almost as soon as the words left his master's lips. Dr. Grenfell let the trace tighten around his hands until the dog reached the pan and climbed onto it.

"Good dog!" he cried in relief. "Now, hold!"

The doctor wrapped the line around his wrist and climbed hand over hand. He arose out of the water and pulled himself a few feet. Brin turned around and released himself from the harness, slipping it over his head.

Dr. Grenfell called to Doc, who had the longest trace. The dog swam toward him. The doctor pointed to the ice pan and commanded the animal to go. As it climbed onto the pan, its master held the line tightly and called for the dog to move. A powerful dog, Doc hauled his master forward.

"Hold it there, Doc!"

He pulled himself to the ice pan and dragged his weary body atop it. He lay face down, exhausted. Turning over, he called the rest of his dogs to him. They came one by one, pulling themselves out of the water and shaking themselves clean of the slob.

"If only I had the komatik," Dr. Grenfell said to Jerry. "All my gear is in it, even my rifle. But how can I get it? If I had a line, maybe I could send one of you back."

As if on cue, the komatik rolled over onto its side, the movement of the sea causing it to overturn. A sick feeling came over Dr. Grenfell and he nearly wept in frustration.

The ice pan on which he stood was comprised of chunks of ice which were beginning to deteriorate. Determined not to give up, he struggled to his feet. His line cabin was not far away, so he shouted for help. After a few minutes he gave up, realizing no one was likely to hear him. He looked at his overturned komatik. Swimming to it was out of the question. He turned his gaze southwest, toward the town of Main Brook. Looking around for another pan, he saw one about a hundred feet away.

"I must make it to that one," he said, fixing the harness on his leader. He took the traces from the other dogs and joined them together to make one long line.

"Okay, Brin," he said. "Get moving!"

Obediently the dog slipped overboard and swam to the ice pan. He soon reached his destination and climbed aboard, then turned and looked expectantly at the doctor.

"Hold it there, Brin!"

Dr. Grenfell pulled tightly on the trace, but the dog held.

"Good dog!" he encouraged.

With that, he threw himself into the water. Resurfacing, he grabbed the trace and pulled himself through the frigid sea. It was a gruelling task. His fingers were starting to numb, and the sticky slob clung to him like paste and hindered his every move. As he inched along, the hundred feet seemed to be a mile, and the five minutes he estimated it would take, an hour.

Brin held firm. The doctor pulled through the rolling sea and reached the ice pan, which he was pleased to discover was more stable than the first. He evaluated his position, casting an inquisitive glance toward the shore. The hairs on the back of his neck bristled when he saw that the wind and tide were pushing him away from the coastline. He scanned the shore and the timber area beyond and determined that he was close to Goose Tickle Point. Unfortunately he was now headed into the ocean. He was now at the mercy of the wind and tide.

The doctor called his dogs, who were still on the first, unstable ice pan, anxiously awaiting a signal. At the sound of his voice, each of them jumped into the slob and swam to him. They joined him on his new perch and shook their coats, spraying slob everywhere. These were large dogs. Dr. Grenfell nervously estimated a total weight of six hundred pounds. Though the ice had sunk significantly under the dogs' weight, he would not order any of them off. He looked around for another surface, but could see none.

"I guess this is our lifeboat," he said to his dogs, looking from one to the other, "and if God permits us to use this one—either to take us to safety or give us a straight passage into eternity—I don't know about you, but I'm willing to accept it."

The English doctor turned and looked out the bay at the ocean. He knew that he would need more than luck to survive this. With eight dogs standing around him, and without a coat, cap, or mitts to ward off the cold, he bowed his head and prayed.

It had been a ghastly day for Charley, too. The skiff bumped as it was dragged over—and through—the ice. A furious tide rip nearly swept the helpless craft into the raging sea. Aided by the brute strength of Allan Hancock's rowing team, however, it stayed in deeper water and away from the undertow.

Every time the boat bumped against an ice pan, Charley moaned in pain. He and the others on board spent a nightmare of a time off Crouse Bight. The wind blew on the edge of the heavy ice, and with the sea rolling the men were almost certain that the boat could capsize. There was, however, no time for thoughts of failure or of watery graves. The crew thought only of Charley, not themselves. Their priority was getting the sick young man to the hospital at St. Anthony, to give him a chance at recovery. With their mitts off, and with sweat rolling down their backs and foreheads, they pulled steadily at the oars. With all odds against them, their calloused hands encouraged the boat toward the eastern point of Crouse Bight.

By 3:00 p.m. the party in the rowboat had almost reached Croque, which is located at Epine Cadoret Inlet. The Croque area has quite a history, although the crew in the small rowboat knew little, if any, of it. In 1766 the world-renowned naturalist Sir Joseph Banks (1743-1820) led an expedition from England to Croque, where he built his headquarters and stayed for three years. His was a thorough expedition. Most plant and animal species were studied. The entire bird population, as well as fish species, were also studied. Capturing caribou, he and his men oversaw a live caribou transplant to England and Holland. Charles Collins, a painter and sketcher, accompanied them and illustrated everything the exhibition investigated.

Allan Hancock's boat ran into a field of ice and came to a crunching halt. The crew could not get close to the shoreline, so they tied the craft to a large, frozen outcrop.

Charley had not moved, but he was wide awake. "Aunt Emmie," he said, "I don't have much pain in my leg now."

"Well, that's good, Charley! Maybe you're getting better." The young midwife could hardly believe her ears. Her patient had gone from excruciating pain to relief in the blink of an eye.

"I hope so," the boy replied.

A few men outside stepped onto the ice while Allan climbed to a higher piece to spy around.

"Boys," he said, "not far ahead is a large lake that runs right across the Croque indraft. We've got to go back a couple of hundred yards and cut around. It's open sailing out there."

"It's all right if we don't get caught out there," said Aaron Reid. He had high cheekbones and the intense gleam in this man's eyes tended to put people on edge. His fingers were crooked and almost every fingernail was deformed from hard work.

"So what?" asked Mark with a shrug. "It doesn't make any difference."

Nobody spoke. They knew that Mark's statement was true. The crew had taken chances all day and were ready to take a thousand more. They boarded the boat and moved off, backtracking around the ice pan and sailing along the Croque indraft. On the other side of Croque, they slowed down and moved cautiously. The ice was a little farther off when they entered White's Arm. They exited the other side, angling through the Fishot Islands.

The crew thought they would be icebound, but luck was with them; the tide had cleared a path. However, Hare Bay was not completely free of ice, and they knew this meant they couldn't cross right away. The ice would have to move off completely before they could attempt to traverse the ten-mile expanse.

Allan Hancock and his crew sat patiently, and waited.

16

Dr. Grenfell drifted out slowly, when he noticed that his ice pan was beginning to swing toward Goose Tickle Point. Caught in a mass of slob, the ice pan wheeled about. He came to within a hundred yards of the shoreline, and right there he made up his mind to swim to shore, through the slob and all. He was about to plunge into the icy depths when the ice pan struck a rock. The icy platform shuddered as a wave lifted it high. The wave dissolved, and the pan struck the rock again. Part of it was jarred loose from the second collision. The wind then pushed him and his dogs farther off the coast.

"So close, but not close enough!" he said, wringing his fists.

The pan was buffeted by the wind and the tide, and now began its dreadful journey toward the open sea. The day was clear, with hardly a cloud gracing the sky. Undoubtedly men were out on their woods paths, hauling firewood and materials to repair wharves and build new boats. Dr. Grenfell sat stoically and looked at the White Hills looming in the distance. His reindeer herds were somewhere on those majestic hills.

"Is it possible," he said, "that one of the herders will see me?"

He gave his ice pan a closer examination. It was not much more than just packed snow with a hard surface. As it was pressed more tightly, the surface appeared to move. With a start, he realized the slab of ice he was sitting on was only five inches thick. He had to move.

He looked and looked for another ice pan large enough to hold him as well as his dog team. A large wave lifted his perch as he scanned the area.

There! He saw what he wanted three hundred feet away.

The doctor conjoined the dog traces, doubting he had enough line to reach the ice beyond, but there was no time to worry. His footing was becoming more precarious by the minute, and he knew that he would be in the water before long. Taking off his skin-boots, he emptied the ice and water from them. He decided against putting them back on. Rolling them up, he tied them to the back of a harness instead.

He pointed. "Go, Brin, go!"

For the first time since Dr. Grenfell's troubles began, the lead dog refused to obey. He repeated the order, but again Brin refused, responding only with an uncertain whimper. The doctor knew that his pan would soon split apart, sending both dogs and master into the freezing water. He called and called—even begged—but the animal steadfastly refused to move.

Grabbing Brin and pointing him toward the ice pan, the doctor threw him onto the slob. Brin simply turned around and pulled himself back onto the ice pan.

THE PRICE PAID FOR CHARLEY

An idea formed in the doctor's mind. His rear-hauling dog, Jack, was a well-trained retriever.

"Okay, Jack," he said, reaching down and grasping a piece of ice. The dog came to life as his master made to toss the ice chunk. Dr. Grenfell pointed to the pan, and the dog's eyes followed his hand.

"Go—get it!" Dr. Grenfell ordered, and he threw the piece of ice with all his might.

The dog leaped from the pan before the ice landed. To the doctor's surprise, the slob held the dog's weight. A small dog, Jack adeptly mounted the distant ice pan. The trace Dr. Grenfell had fashioned by combining each dog's line did reach to the other side, and even allowed a little slack.

"Stay!"

The black retriever obeyed.

"Lie down!"

Jack obeyed again.

Pointing to Jack on the other pan, the doctor said to the rest of the team, "Go to Jack!"

His heart swelled as the dog team moved, en masse, over the ice to their companion. A lump caught in his throat as he watched the proud animals' exodus. Most of the dogs fell through before they reached the retriever, but they plowed their way through. The clear blue sky was the only witness to Dr. Grenfell's moment of triumph.

He looked down to see Brin at his feet. The lead dog had lagged behind while the other six had gone to join Jack. He issued a sharp command, and at last Brin jumped into the slob, bravely starting across. He went through in the wake of the other dogs, floundering as the others had, but he kept moving.

Dr. Grenfell backed to the far side of his disintegrating ice pan. When Brin pulled the line tight, he ran and slid into the slob. Within seconds, he sank to his neck. The dogs on the larger ice pan looked at him curiously. He couldn't move, so he let his lead dog pull the line tight again. To his dismay, the dog stopped, unable to move any farther. Never one to give up, he tied the end of the line securely around his waist and pulled himself along, using the dog as an anchor. When he reached the animal, he let the dog take advantage of the slack to forge ahead.

The English doctor felt something strange happening to him. He was sleepy. He wanted to doze. Struggling to tread water, he felt a heavy lethargy fall over him and thought that he could no longer hold the line tightly enough to drag himself along.

"Hurry, Brin!" he shouted in a quavering voice.

He rose with the waves one moment, peeked out over the ice, and the next sank into the swell. His view alternated between slob ice and the blue sky overhead.

Brin climbed up on the ice pan.

"Lay down!"

The dog shook itself, and obeyed.

Dr. Grenfell slowly and with great difficulty pulled himself alongside the ice pan. Pulling the trace tight with one hand, he placed an arm up on the pan and called to Brin.

"Pull!"

The dog jumped up and pulled. Dr. Grenfell felt himself rise up out of the water, up and up, and flop down onto the frozen slab of ice. He lay there for what seemed an eternity, at once amazed by his team's abilities and humbled by the understated power of the elements.

The ice and slob around him rumbled as the pan bobbed up and down. The swell seemed to be increasing. He struggled to his hands and knees, and water ran from his clothes. Ice was lodged inside his shirt, and his football socks had come off halfway and stuck to the ice. His dogs seemed to be happy enough. They looked at him with complete trust.

Dr. Grenfell sat down. Pulling off a sock, he twisted it together and wrung out the water. He tore his skin-boots from where he had stored them on the harness and struggled to pull them on. Then he stood up.

"The wind is almost gone," he said, "and I can feel the heat from the sun. Maybe I can get dry."

He basked in the sun for some time. He wore a heavy winter shirt made of red and grey material. Inside was his football sweater, which was made of a silky fabric. He decided he would remove the covering shirt and spread it out to dry.

The wind had completely died down. At two-thirty in the afternoon he stood and waved at the White Hills. He could see plainly the Lock's Cove area. He looked southwest toward Brent Islands, half a mile away. Too much slob and ice lay between him and the shoreline to offer any hope of getting ashore. At that moment all hope fled from him. He knelt among his eight dogs and prayed. He put on his shirt, which was warm to the touch, and again felt like falling asleep.

"Am I selfish?" he asked himself, unconsciously dismissing his duties as a doctor, and his present wages, which were non-existent.

"Am I desperate?" He sat upright. Familiar words flashed through his mind. *Don't go near the ice.*

"Yes," said Dr. Grenfell, "I guess it's my own fault. I wouldn't take George's advice. I may be getting what is coming to me . . . but I don't deserve to die."

At three-thirty he felt he was being carried by the tide, driving into the bay and farther toward Lock's Cove. The ice loosened. Openings formed. The sea remained heavy, rumbling in the distance onto Brent Islands. He rested his head on his knees, wondering what he would do when night overtook him.

Peter and Roy arrived at the Lane's Pond camp at six o'clock that evening. Roy's brother Joe was there with his friends, passing the time by trouting through the ice. Roy was glad to see him on his feet again after he had been bedridden from his dangerous journey to gather food for the family. Joe, however, was less than happy when Roy and Peter arrived without the doctor.

"We're responsible, you know," Joe said, "if anything happens to Dr. Grenfell."

"There's not much that could have happened to him," Roy argued. "Maybe he was called back to St. Anthony."

"Don't be silly! If that happened, he would've sent someone to tell us."

Roy threw up his hands and muttered irritably.

THE PRICE PAID FOR CHARLEY

"Maybe Dr. Grenfell is at the bottom of Hare Bay with a broken leg or something, expecting you to come back to get him," Joe pressed. "The people at Lock's Cove won't be out looking for him. They think he's with us."

Peter Lane thought about it. "You could be right, Joe," he said. "Do you know something, boys? Dr. Grenfell went out on that ice, and the wind pitched off northwest. I'd say that he's a goner."

"Never!" said Roy. "Look! We were advised not to go near that ice, and any man with a level head on his shoulders would never go to the edge of that shoreline. The sea was breaking everywhere, boys, even into the bottom of the bay, so rule that out. Dr. Grenfell has more sense than any of us."

"I hope you're right," Joe said in a quiet voice.

"Anyway," Roy continued, "Joseph Ollerhead told us he would go around the bottom of the bay if the doctor didn't show up at his house by four o'clock. He said he's planning to go to St. Anthony for the parade tomorrow, so he might go this evening."

They retired to the cabin and ate a lunch of fried trout. The fresh fish Joe and the others caught were delicious. Roy stood when they finished eating.

"Okay, boys," he said, "let's get ready and go home. 'Tis going to freeze tonight, and I'd say that we should be ready for a funeral when we get home." The meaning of his words was not lost on those sitting at the table.

"I wouldn't say so," Joe countered. "If Charley was dead, there'd be people here looking for us by now."

Roy shrugged. "Maybe you're right." He winked and said, "Certainly by now those old midwives have Charley's leg sawed off."

Peter couldn't help but grin. "Anything's possible," he quipped.

Joe glared at the two of them. "I've never seen anything like it. Ever since Father died, our family has had the town of Englee—and most of the peninsula, for that matter—in an uproar! And here we are now, in the worst mess of all. We've got Dr. Grenfell lost and we don't know what to do."

With that he got up and stalked off to check on the dogs. When he bent to examine them, he saw that they were exhausted. Long, deep lacerations scarred their bodies, no doubt accumulated from a hard day's riding.

"We've got no choice but to leave for home," he said when he returned to the others. They set out for Englee that evening.

"What can I do?" Dr. Grenfell said.

He could not lay down and die. That would be the death of a coward. He needed something on his back to halt the wind. He decided to cut the legs from his skin-boots to make a jacket, or at least part of one. Holding the two pieces of sealskin, he used his knife to stitch them together, using part of the leather trace. He put on the garment, tying the lines over his shoulder and beneath his arms.

His thoughts turned to Charley Hancock. He knew the boy would die if he did not receive medical attention soon. Indeed, the boy could be dead already. "But what can I do?" As he

THE PRICE PAID FOR CHARLEY

looked at the waves around him, the hills and valleys surrounding Hare Bay, the ocean through the bay's entrance, and the sky with all its vastness, Dr. Grenfell felt like an animal in a cage. Although Hare Bay has a surface area of approximately one hundred square miles, he felt like he was trapped in a prison cell.

With his mind on Charley, the doctor prayed. "Dear God, have You a message for me? Then, open my ears and my eyes that I may receive it." He paused. Looking toward the sky, he continued, "And, dear Lord, help me to open my heart and accept Your Will."

He looked at his watch. Five-thirty. He resumed waving at the shore, hoping beyond hope that someone in Lock's Cove would see him, while the sun tipped over the western hills.

III

17

"WHAT AN AWFUL SIN!" Levi Dawe commented to his fellow sealers. "When this cools down we should be able to kill a few young harps," he said, referring to young seals that had been in the water for a month or so.

"I'd say so, too," added Bill Reid.

The Reids and Dawes worked the entire day salvaging most of their seal pelts by pulling them to safer ground. In mid-February the heavy pack ice, known as Arctic ice, arrives on the Great Northern Peninsula, after being pushed south along the Labrador coast. The harp seal herd accompanies the Arctic ice, which stretches out to sea about 200 miles. Adult female harps typically congregate around "whelping" ice near the shore, where their young—whitecoats—are born. While in the area the seals enter the bays in search of food. They were traditionally hunted between mid-March and mid-April. In 1908 the people around the coast depended on seal meat and skins to keep body and soul together. Sealskin was used for clothing, everything from boots to caps to dogs' harnesses, holding-ropes, and a wide variety of household commodities.

For this reason the Lock's Cove resident George Reid, along with his sons, netted seals under the ice at Hare Bay. The movement of the ice, coupled with often tempestuous weather conditions, made it a dangerous job. Their knowledge and understanding of the work, however, usually resulted in a successful harvest.

George Reid was a fisherman, farmer, lumberman, boat builder, and did anything else that needed to be done! Uncle George was called upon whenever a need arose. If any needed advice, they contacted him. He was also an entertainer. His home was the centre of attraction in town. Whoever passed through Lock's Cove called at his place. The Dawes comprised another family in town. Although not a large family, they had enough sons to operate fishing gear comfortably.

The Reids hunted seals in late February and early March, and they did well with their work. They cleaned seals near the shoreline, at the point of land nearest their nets. This limited the distance required to haul their seals—and also avoided a mess of seal paunch and blood near their village. They skinned their catch daily. The skins, with the fat attached, were brought ashore and buried in the snow, thereby keeping them from spoiling.

Levi decided he would climb a nearby cliff, about fifty feet up, to look for seals before he and Bill went home for the day.

"I'd say that by tomorrow noon we might be able to get a boat in the water," he said. "The sea might quiet down by then."

THE PRICE PAID FOR CHARLEY

"Maybe so," Bill responded. "Don't be too long up there, Levi. I'm starving!"

"No, I'm just going to take a look."

Levi scaled the edge of the cliff with ease. When he regained his breath he looked out to sea. The sun was almost in his eyes. A big sea was heaving, but he took his time, scanning slowly for the often elusive harp seal. He looked all the way across the bay.

"Nothing!" he concluded. "Not an eye or ear of anything! I guess the sea must have everything frightened to death!"

He made ready to descend the cliff, but stopped. Something had caught his eye.

"Yes," he said in a low voice, squinting against the evening sun's glare, "something's out there."

Taking a mark with the distant land on the other side of the bay, he leaned against a rock and continued staring at the small speck in the bay, trying to make sense of it.

"It's not a seal," he said slowly. "What is it? It looks like a man . . ."

Levi called to the men below. "Hey, boys!" he shouted. "Come up here! I see something!"

"What do you see?" Bill called.

"I see a man!"

The sealers laughed.

"Listen boys!" continued Levi. "I see something out there on the ice. Come up and take a look!"

They scaled the cliff in a hurry and saw what had captured Levi's attention.

"'Tis nothing but a bunch of tops on a pan of ice, Levi," one of the sealers said.

"No, sir," Levi replied indignantly. "I'm sure I saw a figure stand up. It looks like a man waving his arms."

"Now, Levi, listen!" said Bill, demanding the attention of everyone on the cliff. "At that distance—that's six miles away," he said in a mock-serious tone, "are you sure that you didn't see a fish-fly on his head?"

The other men laughed uproariously.

"You can laugh all you want, but I'm sure that I saw a man out there," Levi said matter-of-factly.

"Come on, Levi, that's a bunch of rubbish the sea hove up, or something. Let's go on home. 'Twill soon be suppertime."

"Boys," Levi insisted calmly, "this is serious. Just suppose it's a man, and we ignore him, and tomorrow we discover that somebody has been driven off."

His words sobered the others. They were not the careless type. Although young, they were a responsible lot and handled most problems in stride. Bill scanned the area, concentrating on the black dot on the icefield. He strained his eyes for a closer look.

"I wonder," he muttered. "I wonder."

"Yes," Levi said slowly, "I bet you're thinking the same thing I am."

The other sealers looked at each other uneasily.

"Listen," said Bill, "we don't have much time before the sun goes down. 'Tis about six o'clock now. I'm going for the old man's glass."

THE PRICE PAID FOR CHARLEY

"Why all the rush?" asked his younger brother.

Bill turned to him quickly.

"That could be Dr. Grenfell out there!"

"Well, no," his brother said, "Dr. Grenfell didn't go on the ice this day. I heard the old man telling him this morning not to go on the ice."

"We can't take the chance," Bill countered, waving a hand impatiently. "We have to find out if someone is out there. It doesn't matter who it is."

"Okay. Let's go!"

The two Reid boys descended the cliff and ran for their dog team. Quickly untangling them, they sped away.

Night was coming and Dr. Grenfell knew he had to make preparations. He took the harnesses from his dogs and cut the bindings, which were strips of cloth two to three inches wide. The harnesses used on the Great Northern Peninsula, and indeed throughout Newfoundland, were homemade. The ropes were nine- thread bass, six to seven feet long, depending on the size of the dog.

With the bass rope exposed, the doctor decided to make a stuffing for his socks, a trick he had learned after observing the three Laplander families who tended to his reindeer herd on the White Hills. When preparing to go to the hills that winter, they placed their bare feet into their boots and stuffed grass inside for insulation. It must have worked because they never complained of frostbite. He cut the bass rope into small pieces and made oakum out of the rope, then stuffed his football socks with the material. Next he took the binding strips he had taken off the harnesses and wound them tightly around his legs from the ankles up.

He was still cold. The ice pan was too small and fragile to allow him to exercise, so that was out of the question. His biggest problem was that he got wet every time he sat down.

"I can't get my blood circulating. If only I had something to sit on," he said, "I could huddle between the dogs. What can I do?"

He stood and waved again absentmindedly. The sun, hanging in the western sky, reached low for the hills and the dense forest of the Main Brook area. He looked affectionately at his dogs, and a sudden thought struck him.

"No," he said slowly, "I can't."

Try as he might, though, he could think of no other alternative. He knew well the severity of frostbite. When he came to Newfoundland and Labrador, he had heard scores of hair-raising stories about the suffering of both young and old alike. One such story involved a girl who lived on the Labrador coast. She had gotten lost and had spent a bitterly cold winter night outdoors. When she was found in the morning, both of her feet and part of her legs were frozen. The youngster was sure to die unless medical help was found. Unfortunately none was available. Local remedies were applied, but infection set in soon after. The girl's father examined her and knew that one of two things had to be done. Either he would have to let his girl die, or both of her legs would have to be amputated. He talked it over with the rest of his family, and they decided on the latter course. When Dr. Grenfell arrived at the town, he had found the girl in a sorrowful state. She was rushed to the St. Anthony hospital, where she was restored to health, minus her legs.

One by one, he called his dogs by name. Brin, Doc, Moody, Watch, Spy, Sue, Jerry, and Jack huddled around him.

"How can I do this?" he pondered. "Will I start with the oldest and work my way to the youngest?"

He looked around him and saw he was near the centre of the bay, but closer to the Main Brook area to the southwest. Standing once more, he again waved his half-hearted plea to the outlying hills. He looked at his dogs, hardly believing what he was about to do. A doctor by profession, he knew what it was to cut through living tissue. He had performed surgical incisions on living flesh, even amputations, but only to save the lives it belonged to. Now he would have to kill. Even worse, he would have to kill his dogs with their comrades looking on. He wondered how they would react; he knew there was no place to hide.

Every passing second was a new chill in his bones, so he made up his mind to kill a dog right away. By now his feet were getting cold and his hands were numb. Soon he would not have the strength to do what was necessary. At least he would have something to sit on, he thought horribly.

Earlier in the day he had noticed that the dogs seemed hungry. The traces, made out of sealskin, would serve as a treat for them. He rolled the traces into a coil and hung it on his belt, suspecting he would need it before the night was over.

He selected Moody, a dog he especially loved. This dog had

been with him from a pup. "I never thought, Moody," he said with tears in his eyes, "that I would ever have to kill you to help me stay alive, and maybe I am only making your end a little quicker than mine." He scratched the dog's ears affectionately and said, "Forgive me, Moody."

Dr. Grenfell counted Moody's ribs and expertly moved his finger between them, where he would insert the instrument of death. Leading the dog a couple of steps away, he turned his back to the others. He took the leather traces off his waist, made a loop at the end, and threw it over the dog's head. Fearing the others would tackle Moody if he howled, the doctor made him lie down before bringing the line tight with his feet. As he did, he plunged his knife into the dog's heart, to the handle. He left the knife in to prevent blood from escaping and making a mess of the pelt. Moody struggled and managed to loosen the line just enough to give his master a wicked bite on the leg.

Within moments, Moody lay dead at the doctor's feet. A few of the other dogs raised their heads. He deftly skinned the dog and placed its carcass near the edge of the ice pan. His hands were beginning to warm, but his feet were still freezing. "I guess I'll have to make some kind of rug to go over me," he said, "which means I'll have to kill another dog."

The next dog he chose was Watch, the one with the golden setter coat and ever-tearful eyes. He was the youngest member of Dr. Grenfell's team. The dog voluntarily walked to the side of the ice pan where the body of his comrade lay, not knowing that he would soon follow. Dr. Grenfell applied the same method, but held more firmly to Watch to prevent another bite. After skinning the dog, he used his knife and part of the skin trace to sew together the two pelts. He sat on one, with the other covering his back.

His feet were still cold, and they were beginning to lose all sensation. After a moment of agonized indecision, the doctor realized he would have to take another dog's life. This time he chose Spy.

He led the animal to what he grimly referred to as the butchering area. Quickly putting the loop over Spy's head, he counted the ribs. He placed the dog on his side and, while pulling the trace tightly, pierced the animal's heart. The dog went wild, floundering and howling, but eventually he went limp. Dr. Grenfell skinned the dog and sewed the pelt onto the other two, making a full-sized rug of sorts, capable of covering his whole body.

The sun prepared to sink below the horizon. Dr. Grenfell lay down, exhausted, and pulled his makeshift rug over him. He wondered if he would survive the night, or if what he had just done would only prolong the inevitable. With this thought, he bowed his head and wept.

Aaron Reid spent hours searching in vain for an opening large enough to row across Hare Bay. The ice moved in and out of the bay as the sun gave him and his crewmates long shadows. The rough sea broke over nearby shoals and sent large pieces of Arctic ice hurtling against the cliffs, where thunderous booms reverberated for long, terrifying minutes at a time.

They eventually entered Maiden's Arm, a tiny harbour located a mile down the headland from the Fishot Islands. On his map of 1765, Sir Joseph Banks had called this sheltered and well-wooded haven Prince Edward Harbour. Aaron Reid's crew knew they would need to stop here; attempting to cross to Hare Bay in these nighttime conditions would be suicidal. They moved the boat behind the island and went ashore.

The men pulled the skiff, with Charley and Emmie still aboard, out of the water. They lit two lanterns and, with the boat's sail, fashioned a lean-to over the craft. A fire was started, and Allan Hancock fetched a kettle. Emmie, the young midwife, leaned over the fire and told the men that one of Charley's abscesses had broken. Pus was trickling down his leg and up his back, she said.

"There's a hole in his leg big enough to put your fist in," she explained. "If we can only get him to a doctor! We've got twenty miles to go yet."

Little did she know that, less than four miles away, a doctor with frozen hands and feet sat wrapped in dog-skins on an ice pan, shivering in the moonlight and hugging his snarling husky dogs while they sniffed the bodies of their three dead friends.

18

BILL REID RETURNED WITH a spyglass just as the sun was making its final descent. He and his brother dashed to the cliff where Levi Dawe was waiting.

"Do you know what that is, Bill?" The younger Reid brother pointed, his eyes wide. "It's a man with a bunch of dogs! I see him!"

Bill caught his breath after the short climb and opened the spyglass. The telescopic glass, made entirely of brass, was perhaps a hundred years old and belonged to their father, George. Bill put it to his eye and adjusted it.

"Ah, yes," he said. "I've got it!"

"Well, what is it?" Levi asked anxiously.

"It's Dr. Grenfell!"

"Let me have a look."

Bill handed him the glass. Levi steadied his arm, then peered through the instrument.

"I see him!" he declared. "You're right, 'tis a man! Nine out of ten I'd say 'tis Dr. Grenfell!"

Levi handed the glass to Bill's brother, who took a turn and agreed that Dr. Grenfell was drifting out of Hare Bay on an ice pan. And now the sun was going down.

"Hand me that glass again," Levi said. "I want to see something." He looked out the bay for a few seconds, then snapped the spyglass shut. "Just what I thought!" he exclaimed.

"You thought what?" Bill asked. He appeared shaken and his face was white.

"Here, Bill, have a look."

Bill took the instrument again.

"Do you see him?"

"Got him! "

"Now, tell me what Dr. Grenfell is sitting on," Levi said.

For a moment Bill was silent.

"He's on nothing . . . nothing but the slob," he said slowly. "I don't even see a komatik. Look! He's sitting on nothing but the slob!"

"Let's get a boat and go out," Levi suggested as they hurried to the dogs.

The men went to George Reid's house and found him near the woodpile. He watched them approach. When Bill had come for the telescope, he told his father that they had seen a man on the ice, driving out the bay. George had been uneasy. He knew Dr. Grenfell was a risk taker, but he hadn't dreamed that the doctor would take this one. Jumping off the two dog teams, the young men ran to Uncle George.

"Uncle George!" Levi shouted. "It's Dr. Grenfell! We saw him plain, and he's just in his shirt sleeves!"

THE PRICE PAID FOR CHARLEY

George was stunned.

"Old man," Bill said to his father, "he's not even on a pan of ice. He's sitting on the slob and waving like mad. I'd say he's about three miles from the point, and in line with the springs."

"Do you think we should launch the punt? Make a beeline for him?" asked Levi.

"No," George said. "It'll be dark in twenty minutes, and there's so much sea. We'll all be drowned. It's going to take an hour to get a boat ready anyway, so listen, boys. Dr. Grenfell is going to have to spend the night on the ice. Get your supper quickly and come to the house."

George turned and walked to his house as the young men stood transfixed with tears in their eyes. Dr. Grenfell was their doctor, their clergyman, their hope, and they each felt like they were abandoning him.

The night fell on Dr. Grenfell like a giant cloak. The bloody skins of his three dead dogs clung to him, hugging every curve of his body. As he lay wrapped from head to toe, he felt the constant movement of the ice as the sea heaved upward and settled again. The ice shifted, and he knew it was possible that the patch of ice on which he lay could fall apart without warning. He turned on his side, and looking north toward Lock's Cove, he thought he detected a light. He stood up as the next wave lifted him.

"Yes," he said, "it's a light from one of the houses."

The doctor suspected the light came from George Reid's

house, where he had slept the night before and received such great hospitality. He could almost visualize the table being set, the smiling face of Mrs. Reid, the comfortable bed in which he had slept. Then the rumble of the sea and his dogs' breathing awoke him from his reverie, bringing the reality of his situation home with a crushing weight. The oily smell of the dog-skins against his cheek turned his stomach. His feet stung from the cold. He dared not kick or jump to get his blood circulating, for fear of splitting the pan. As long as the slob chunks stayed close, he stood a chance.

Dr. Grenfell's mind was in turmoil. He recalled that he had told his nurse to advise his driver, Reuben Simms, that he would not be returning for two days.

"But I might be out here for longer than that," he despaired.

An idea came to him. "My matchbox! If it's dry, maybe I can get a fire going. But what can I burn?"

He thought his rope would suffice, so he cut off a piece and made oakum from it, pulling it apart and collecting the loose fibres. To this he added fat from the dead dogs' intestines. Hoping against hope, he struck a match. It refused to light.

With a sigh the doctor took the rope's fibres and stuffed them inside his shirt. He beckoned his dogs to lay near him to lend him some body heat. If the dogs were to attack him, he knew, his only defence would be his sheath knife. He kept his hand near it at all times.

After midnight the doctor felt drowsy. The wind had disappeared and a calm had settled over Hare Bay. In the solitude

THE PRICE PAID FOR CHARLEY

the words of an old hymn which he had sung as a boy at his church in London rang in his head.

My God, my Father, while I stray,
Far from my home on life's dark way,
Oh, teach me from my heart to say,
Thy Will be done.

The words awakened memories of his boyhood days, days when his dear mother cooked his meals, made his bed, cared for him, days when his father took him into the countryside, days when his brother showed him how to catch trout in the river. He fell into a fitful sleep and dreamed strange dreams of old men and wild dogs perishing in unforgiving northern climes.

19

A CROWD BEGAN TO gather at George's house. He sent a man to follow Dr. Grenfell's tracks, to see where the doctor went astray, and he dispatched another man on dog team to tell the people in Goose Cove that the doctor was driving out the bay on the slob. George instructed them be on the lookout for him at daybreak.

That done, he sent for Nat Dawe and George Andrews. Shortly, the men joined him in his parlour and sat at the table.

"Don't let anyone in here while we're talking," George told his wife. "We've got to make plans."

She nodded and assured them that they would be left alone.

"We're in quite a mess, men," he began, "and we don't have many choices. I don't understand Dr. Grenfell. I practically begged him not to go near the ice."

"I guess the problem is not what Dr. Grenfell has done, but what we're going to do tonight or tomorrow morning," offered Nat.

THE PRICE PAID FOR CHARLEY

"I don't see much hope at all," said Mr. Andrews. "The boys said he was on the bare slob. As soon as the wind slacks, all that stuff is going to fall apart—and down he'll go! Slouse!"

"You're right," said Nat.

"We know that," George said impatiently, "but we've got to do something."

"You won't do anything this night," Nat warned. "There's too much sea. It'll be impossible to launch a boat in the darkness."

George nodded in agreement.

Nat continued. "Now let's look at a few points. Let's see what Dr. Grenfell has against him and what he's got in his favour. First, let's suppose he's on something that can stand his weight and keep him up.

"What does he have going against him? Number one is the wind. He can get pushed around the bay and out to the ocean. Number two is the tide. Suppose that after the wind dies out the tide wheels around and pushes him to the shore. You know that everything will be beaten to pieces."

"And thirdly," interrupted Mr. Andrews, "it's the cold. This is going to be a cold night and, according to the boys, he doesn't have anything on. If he doesn't drown, he'll freeze."

They heard someone enter the room.

"Uncle George?"

"Yes," George Reid said, turning to the man.

"I followed the tracks Dr. Grenfell made this morning. He only went a couple of miles before he hauled his komatik onto the ice."

Mr. Andrews spoke up. "I'd say he made a straight jab for Brent Islands."

"Maybe you're right," said George. "But where are the two fellows from Englee? Maybe they went out on the ice, too. If Dr. Grenfell didn't meet them, they would be back here looking for him, wouldn't they?"

"I don't know," Nat said. "At daylight we've got to have a boat ready. It looks like the sea is going to keep up. We're going to have a pretty good night, I think, but if it starts to snow, we'll never see the doctor."

George nodded. "Yes, we should get a boat."

"Nat has the real boat for that," Mr. Andrews said, "and she's new, too!"

"Yes," said Nat, "we'll take mine. She's tight as a cup and ready to go. All we've got to do is get her in the water."

"How many men do we need in her?" George asked.

"We'll need two sets of oars and a man on each. That'll be four men rowing, with a fifth in the rear, watching and steering. Five men should be able to pull her over any heavy ice."

"You're right."

"I can't go. I've got a bad hand, so I won't be able to grip the oar. But if nobody else will go," he said with a grin, "one arm is better than neither one."

George laughed. "We don't expect you to go with that hand. We'll get a crew."

"I'll go," Mr. Andrews volunteered. He was a short but strong man who worked hard as a fisherman and logger. He was fearless at thirty-five years old, a family man, and the best of seamen. "Nat," he continued, "I'll go in charge of the crew. Ask Levi if he'll go, will you?"

"There's no problem," Nat said. "Levi will go. You've got your crew. That'll be yourself, George here, Bill and young Levi, and my Levi. Is that it?"

"Yes," said Mr. Andrews, "that's it."

"Okay. Let's get some men and fit out the punt."

George Reid held up a hand. "Just a moment, Nat. We've got a job to do—you and me—so we should give Mr. Andrews here the task of getting the crew ready."

"All right," said Nat. He turned to address Mr. Andrews. "Get Levi and Walter. They know where everything is. Make sure you have enough thole-pins and oars."

"Now, Nat," George said when Mr. Andrews left, "I think we should send a dog team to Main Brook to see Joseph Ollerhead. He'll know if the two fellows from Englee are with Dr. Grenfell or not. For sure they stopped at his place on their way through."

"Yes," said Nat, "I guess you're right. But if Dr. Grenfell went off the ice and they didn't know it, why haven't they come back here to see where he is? And, if they know that he's out on the ice, why didn't they come back here to let us know earlier?"

"That's what I've been telling you, Nat. Maybe they're out there somewhere!"

"But, on the other hand, maybe they're over on the other side of the bay trying to get out to him."

"Maybe," George said. "Either way, we should send a team to Joseph's to check it out."

"'Tis funny that Joseph hasn't passed through here. He usually goes to the Orange Lodge in St. Anthony."

"There's no meeting in St. Anthony tomorrow. Only in Griquet."

"I know," said Nat, "but that's all the same to Joseph. He doesn't miss one, no matter where it is."

George nodded. "We should also put someone on the hill tonight to check on the wind and tide. After midnight the moon will be up, and these people should get a clear view of the bay. This will give us a rough idea of where Dr. Grenfell will be after daylight."

"Let's put four men there," Nat said. "Two to each shift. I'll be in charge of that."

Rachel Reid entered the room and, before she spoke, George noticed his wife had been crying.

"George," she said, "Joseph Ollerhead just arrived. He's out tying on his dogs. "

"Good. We won't have to send anyone to Main Brook now. Rachel, get a cup of tea ready for him."

Rachel went into the kitchen.

"The moment I find out some details," said Nat, "I'll get going and round up a crowd."

They heard a commotion in the porch as Joseph Ollerhead and his wife came in. Mrs. Ollerhead was crying, and when she saw Rachel, the two women collapsed weeping into each other's arms.

"What are we going to do, Aunt Rachel?" sobbed Mrs. Ollerhead. "Dr. Grenfell is gone! He's drowned!"

"The two of you, knock it off!" Joseph barked. "Rachel, where's George?"

"I'm in here, Joseph," George called.

"George," Joseph began, shaking his head as he burst through the door, "what in the world is going on? Is it true that someone saw Dr. Grenfell out on the ice?"

"Yes, 'tis true. The boys saw him just before dark. He's driving out the bay, and to make matters worse, he's on nothing but the slob!"

"You talk about!" Joseph exclaimed.

"Joseph," said Nat, "did you see Peter Lane or Roy Hancock anywhere between here and Main Brook?"

"Yes, they came to my place today. I told them that Dr. Grenfell must have been called back to St. Anthony or something, so they went home."

"It's too bad they didn't come back here and let us know. We might have been able to get out before dark."

"Those fellows would not have made it here before dark," Joseph explained. "Their dogs were cut to pieces. It took me four hours to get here."

"At least we've got only one to rescue, then," George reasoned.

"Do you have your plans made?" Joseph asked.

"Just about," answered Nat.

"What can I do? Do you want me to go on to St. Anthony and get the boys ready to move in the morning?"

"No," George said. "If there's a big crowd, and they go out there in boat tomorrow morning, somebody could be drowned, especially with the sea as bad as it is."

"Okay," replied Joseph, "so we'll stay here the night."

"Yes, that's the best thing to do."

"I should get going," said Nat. "I'll be back in a couple of hours and I'll keep you fellows informed."

When Nat went outside, George turned to Joseph. "What do you think of it?" he asked.

"Dr. Grenfell can be rescued if he doesn't do anything crazy," Joseph said after a moment's thought. "If he has nothing to wrap around him, he'll have a rough night, but he won't freeze to death. What I mean by doing something foolish is trying to get ashore in the night, by walking on the slob, or something."

"He won't do that."

"I don't know. He went out on ice that wasn't fit for anything, so he just might decide to start for shore out there." He shook his head. "These Englishmen, George! I don't know about them. My son, Dr. Grenfell has too much on his mind. He hasn't got time to go in around the bay. He's prepared to take any risk just to save time."

"I don't know about that, Joseph. He stopped here last night and had prayers in the schoolhouse."

"That's a different matter, George. Seems like he's got lots of time for that."

"I figure that Dr. Grenfell is in for a rough time of it tonight. I know I wouldn't want to be out there with a bunch of husky dogs."

"You're right, there," Joseph said. "The other day when Reuben Simms came through Main Brook, he had to have the whip in his hands all the time. These dogs were crazy."

THE PRICE PAID FOR CHARLEY

George nodded. "It looked like he could handle the team. I watched him when he left. He had them under control."

Aunt Rachel brought in tea for the men as George continued. "It's not the dogs he's got to watch out for, but his own self."

Joseph grunted as he sipped his hot tea.

"There's one thing I think the boys should do," George went on. "They should go up on the hill and light the tar barrel. Dr. Grenfell will get some courage when he sees the fire. He'll know for sure that we know he's out on the ice, so that'll keep him going."

"If I was out there and saw a fire on land," Joseph argued, "I'd think there was someone signalling for me to come to shore. If we do that Dr. Grenfell might start walking in, especially if he thinks he's on his way out to sea."

George sighed. "Maybe you're right," he said.

At that moment, Mr Andrews came in and sat at the table.

"We've got the boat up and out of the snow, and we're getting her ready," he reported. "We're going to have to borrow some oars."

"No problem," said George. "Make sure you put a hammer, nails, oakum, and corking iron on board. And something to repair her," he added.

"The boys are at that now. They're also getting a galley ready."

Later that night, Nat went out to the cliff. At midnight he returned to report the weather to George.

"There's a big ride on, George," he said. "The ice is running mad, and 'tis severely cold. I'd say 'tis twenty below. But the moon is just coming up, so we'll see better in awhile. 'Tis going to be a light night."

George thanked him, and with that the two men left the house to help the others prepare for the boat trip that would take them on one of the most important search-and-rescue missions ever undertaken in Newfoundland. Dr. Grenfell, who was the backbone and moral support for the people on the Great Northern Peninsula, was in great danger, and though many doubted the doctor would survive the night, each man was willing to lay down his life to give him a fighting chance.

20

MOONBEAMS LIT THE BOILING tide rips which scattered the ice in and around Hare Bay. A dog too cold and miserable to sleep let out a restless howl, triggering a reaction from the human form laying on the rapidly disintegrating chunk of ice that bobbed up and down in the swirling surge of the Arctic current. The man jolted and tried to rise, but he found he was held fast. The animal skins that covered him might as well have been a casket.

After a time he lifted the cover and opened his eyes. The realization of his location flooded into him as the powerful agony of the day stabbed his eyes. The huge dog he had lain with tore itself from his grip and struggled to its feet. The doctor's eyes bulged. He saw the dark, rippling water of the North Atlantic all around him. He had lived to see daylight once again.

Dr. Grenfell pried open the frozen dog-skins and sat up. He had slept for three hours, but only because his exhausted body had demanded it. Now he saw that his ice pan had fallen apart, and the piece on which he and his dogs lay floated forlornly in the middle of a lake that had formed between the outlying icefields. The nearest piece of the icy "mainland" lay several hundred feet from his frozen island. The doctor looked at the sky and was momentarily dazed. He nearly swooned as he realized that his mind had tricked him.

"It's the moon!" he said. "Not the sun!" In a shaky voice he cried, "Dear Lord, help me!"

An excruciating stab of pain hit his extremities, and his hand throbbed. One hand he had placed near the warm body of a dog, but the other had been bared to Jack Frost's cruel breath. His eyes blurred as he stared at it, hoping for some feeling to return. He pried himself into a sitting position and tried to move his fingers, but they didn't respond.

"My hand is frozen!" he rasped. "I'm finished!"

The doctor started to panic. He looked into the eyes of the dog nearest to him, desperately seeking an answer to his problem, but in his sickened heart he knew it was too late to save his hand.

Or was it?

Some memory from his recent trip to Roddickton tried to assert itself. Dr. Grenfell had gone to perform a routine surgery on Charley's leg, but he had also learned something important from the Hancock family, something he thought would come in handy at a later time. He tried to recall his conversation with Charley's brothers.

Do you have any problems with your hands or feet?
No, Doctor.

THE PRICE PAID FOR CHARLEY

Mark, what you went through is nothing short of superhuman. I've heard the stories. Charley is from the same bloodline as you, so I am sure he will survive the operation.

Brin, the leader of his dog team, shifted a little. The doctor looked at the dog, and his eyes widened.

You know, I would have lost my hands if it wasn't for Aunt Lizzie...

"My jingles, that's it!" he cried.

He shuffled to the edge of the ice pan and thrust his hand into the salty murk, recalling Mark Hancock's remedy for frostbite. He couldn't feel anything at first, and if he hadn't been looking at his hand he wouldn't have believed it was immersed in the frigid water. He left it there for a moment, then withdrew it. It felt cold when he tucked it beneath his arm. A searing pain shot through his hand.

"It's starting to awaken," he noted. He tried to move his fingers again and this time they responded.

One of his dogs walked to the stack of animal carcasses he had skinned. As the dog moved, Dr. Grenfell felt the ice pan vibrate under its weight. Knowing that he would not survive if he were forced to swim, he commanded the dog to lay down, and it obeyed.

"If the swell goes down," he said, "maybe the sea will freeze over and I can walk ashore." He was still close enough to shore that a southwest or northeast wind could move him within reach of land. But this was wishful thinking.

"What can I do?" he asked as his breath steamed in the cold night air and his ice pan lifted and dropped threateningly.

He was very thirsty. All around him the salt water teased and tempted him, daring him to take a drink. Crawling back inside the dogs' pelts, an emergency plan began to form in his mind.

"That's what I'll have to do. I don't have any other choice."

From inside his dogskin tent, he called his dogs to lay near him, but now they ignored his plea, as if they themselves sensed danger. He shivered miserably in his makeshift lean-to, dreading the choice he knew he would have to make before long.

Emmie Fillier was known as the mother of Roddickton. At nineteen her hands were calloused from hard toil and her hair was snow-white from the stresses of a few short years of going beyond the call of duty, struggling through winter snowdrifts, bringing children into the world, and relieving mothers of intense pain. Now the young woman faced a crisis. Her patient, dying of tuberculosis, was ice- and rock-bound at the edge of the raging North Atlantic. She stood in the combined light of a winter's moon and a coal-oil lantern, trying to warm her hands near a smoky fire. Her companions were six burly men who were among the toughest who had ever stepped into boots. Indeed, these pioneers had founded the town of Roddickton. They shared a great respect for Emmie and guarded her with their lives.

"'Twill soon be getting daylight," one man commented.

"Yes, it seems that way," his friend replied.

"I wonder what it's like outside."

Aaron Reid spoke up. "I don't know, but I suspect a solid jam."

THE PRICE PAID FOR CHARLEY

"The ice should be loose," said Allan Hancock.

"I know one thing," said Aaron. "The sea hasn't gone back any, if the noise out there is any indication."

Emmie interrupted them. "Let's have a cup of tea and fill the hot water bottles," she said.

Allan nodded. "What do you think of Charley this morning, Emmie?"

"I'm afraid to say," the young midwife replied, "because he seems to be a little worse every hour. I don't know how long we can stay here. I'm afraid he'll catch pneumonia."

"It's a hard spot we're in, Emmie, and last night was a cold one. Only for the sea heaving, we would have been frozen in here this morning. Who's got the time?"

Will Hancock, brother to Charley and Mark, looked at his pocket watch. "'Tis five o'clock, boys."

Aaron looked at the eastern sky. "If Dr. Grenfell was at Englee last night, he'll probably be back in St. Anthony before we get there."

"Not if the ice is off and the paddles stay in the water," said Mark, anxiously shifting his weight from one foot to the other.

"Let's get geared to move," Allan said. "Leave the fire burning just in case we've got to return, and make sure all the tools are picked up. Each man knows what he's responsible for."

The heat from the Waterloo stove permeated the room while George Reid sat at the window looking at the moon through the heavily frosted glass.

"Looks like we're going to have a good day," he mused.

"I hope so," said Bill as he finished his breakfast.

The crew that had been assigned to go in the boat had been told to meet with Nat Dawe and Joseph Ollerhead at George Reid's home at 5:00 a.m. Their plan was in place, but George wanted to finalize everything before they set out. He wanted to go over every detail, and to get a report on the ice, wind, and sea from Nat, who had been sent to the cliff.

Nat arrived, caked in frost, ten minutes ahead of schedule. He sat and extended his hands over the stove.

"A cold night!" he muttered. "If Dr. Grenfell was in his shirt sleeves, he had a rough night."

"You've got that right," Bill said.

"There's one good thing about this cold," said George. "It'll keep the slob frozen together."

Nat chuckled. "I don't know. I think I'd rather drown than freeze to death. At least a fellow would go quickly!"

Bill grinned.

Levi Dawe, Mr. Andrews, and the others arrived and sat at the table. Aunt Rachel cleared it and wiped the oilcloth covering before George spread a large piece of brown wrapping paper across it. The boat crew crowded around the table and saw that it was an old map of Belvy Bay, which had changed its name to Hare Bay at the turn of the century.

"I want an update from Nat on the ice conditions first," George said.

Nat cleared his throat. "I just came from the cliff. There was a job to see anything because of the frost in the air, but there's not a breath of wind out there right now. The ice went apart, then the tide moved in overnight. There's a lot of heavy ice on this side, but as far as we could see in the area where Dr. Grenfell was yesterday evening, the ice has moved out of the bay and is probably off the Fishot Islands by now. The ice didn't come into the bay, that's for sure. At one point—around three o'clock—we heard an awful racket of sea and ice smashing together. I talked it over with the men on watch and they agreed, after eying the ice all night, that Dr. Grenfell must be outside the bay or near the mouth.

"You're going to have a lot of difficulty getting out of here with all this ice around. Launch the boat over it. It's hard ice—the real stuff that can punch a hole in the her. The whole area appears to be moving, so 'tis going to be tricky to get her through it, and it's like that for about a mile and a half."

He picked up a large carpenter's pencil and said, "I think Dr. Grenfell is here." He placed an "X" on the map along the line of land between Goose Cove Cape and the Fishot Islands, but closer to the latter. "I'd say he's here, because the tide is running up.

"You could be right," said Joseph Ollerhead. "You watched the ice, so you should know."

"Now," continued Nat, "here's what I think. Given the severe frost last night, and the fact that Dr. Grenfell had no clothes, I'd say that you're going to pick up a corpse this morning. The only thing we're going to have to look for are his dogs. If Dr. Grenfell is still on the ice, dead or alive the dogs won't leave him. If he falls off the dogs will head for the shore somewhere. I'll be up on the cliff with the glass, and we'll be watching you at all times. If we see him and you're not going straight, we'll fire a rifle shot. That'll be one shot to keep left, and two to keep right. If you don't hear anything, keep going on your course.

"Joseph," he said, "When it gets daylight I want you to get another boat and a crew ready to take off in case the others run into trouble. Just give the signal if you need help."

"That'll be a good thing," George said approvingly.

"Now, George, take a piece of cloth," Nat went on. "If Dr. Grenfell is dead when you get to him, put up a flag half-mast when you come in. That should just about do it. I'll head back to the cliff as soon as you're ready to push off."

George Reid lowered his head and the others watched in silence as tears fell from his face.

"We've got a job to do, boys," the old man said in a broken voice. "I picked you, not because you are the best in this little town, but because I know that you'll do as you're told. There's only one thing I want you to remember. Even though we're searching for a man who ignored danger and went against our advice, we owe our lives to this man. For the first time on the Great Northern Peninsula, people have had relief from pain and a place to rest their sick frames—and it's all thanks to Dr. Grenfell! Think of the thousands yet unborn that we can save if we bring him in alive.

"So remember, when we push off there'll be no danger too great that we can't take!"

An excited murmur of agreement went through the crowd.

THE PRICE PAID FOR CHARLEY

"Let's go," said Nat. "It's getting daylight."

The men stood, but Aunt Rachel held up her hand.

"Just a minute!"

She looked at her husband and two sons, then at the others.

"For a moment," she said, "I want to pray and ask God to give you protection. You know that if Dr. Grenfell was here he'd want it that way. So please, for a moment I want you to bow your heads and listen to me."

"Dear God," she said with emotion, "You know that Dr. Grenfell is out on the ice, and You know about the night he's had. You also know about the work that Dr. Grenfell has been doing, and that it's not finished. I've been praying all night, and You have heard me. I know You have." She tapped the table with her fist. "There's something that I want You to do, God," she continued. "Protect this crew and grant me that none of them will be harmed. Lord, I'm not going to say amen until the doctor sets his feet on the land. I know that You can do it."

"Okay, men," George said after a moment of silence. "Let's go."

With all of the Great Northern Peninsula's hopes resting on their shoulders, the men left the house and headed for the ocean.

21

THE MOON SOARED DAUNTLESS in the heavens, and one can be sure that this most majestic of celestial bodies carried different meanings to the millions of people who beheld it. No doubt young lovers were warmed by tropical breezes and moved to romance within her light, while elsewhere in the world old-timers sat on porches and gazed reverently at her bountiful glow, reminiscing of days gone by that will never return. In northern Newfoundland, in the early moonlit hours of Tuesday, April 21, 1908, an ice pan bobbed up and down in the rolling swell of the ocean bearing a cargo of human flesh and dog meat. The English doctor Wilfred Grenfell was a fighter, a survivor who was up against the biggest challenge of his life as every passing moment warmth was leached from his body and scattered into the night.

Hypothermia was setting in, and he was powerless to stop it. He moved his legs slowly and continuously, as if bicycling, and flexed his fingers and wrists. The hand that had been frozen still pained him, but he was grateful that he could still feel it.

THE PRICE PAID FOR CHARLEY

I wonder what happened to the two fellows from Englee, he thought. *Surely they have alerted someone that I haven't shown up at the cabin, or at Main Brook.* The thought didn't bring him much hope. He figured that if someone were looking for him they would have found him by now. *I have to get ashore on my own*, he concluded.

The doctor thought about his missionary venture in Newfoundland and Labrador, and the Newfoundland government, who at times had not been kind to him. *Why, I wonder? I have been helping the sick, the suffering, and the destitute. I'm not doing it for personal gain. However,* he amended, *they did give me a licence to operate, and a place to cut timber.*

His five dogs started to howl. Struggling, he lifted his dogskin blanket and peeked out. The eastern sky was lightening with a promised sunrise. He gazed at the first flicker of sunlight on the White Hills and prayed, thanking God that He had seen fit to let him live through the night. "If I am rescued sometime today," he prayed, "I will still be able to continue my medical mission. I'll put this behind me as a delay in our progress! Lord, if You spare my life, I will give You the glory and tell it wherever I go. Amen."

Dr. Grenfell crawled out from under the dog-skins. He rolled onto the ice and attempted to stand, but he didn't have the strength. Bracing himself against the ice, he pushed. He was dismayed to note that his hands were sticking to it. Tearing them free, he collapsed, nearly striking his head on a clumper in the process.

The doctor pushed himself to a sitting position and faced

the morning sun. Its rays hurt his eyes, and it was too early yet to get any real comforting warmth from it, but he allowed himself to begin to feel hope. His dogs wagged their tails spiritedly and came near. Vapour rose from their mouths like steam from a kettle. One of the dogs licked his face and the doctor realized that he had been crying.

He stared at the distant shoreline toward Lock's Cove and visualized the people—his friends—sitting down to breakfast. Waves of hunger rolled over him and his mouth was parched. He had to remove the thought from his mind. Looking at the three dog carcasses, he made an awful resolution: it appeared he would have to fall back on his emergency plan after all. A few days earlier, he had read Fridtjof Nansen's book, *Farthest North*. In it, the author described a personal experience wherein dogs had been killed and their blood drunk to ensure human survival.

"I will stick it out until four o'clock. If we are not rescued by then, we will have dog meat."

He looked into Brin's watery eyes, then quickly looked away.

The little boat from Englee battled the ice and heavy sea. The crew could not go through the new ice, or too near the shore, for fear of the breaking sea around the shallow water. They had no choice but to stay in the heavy ice and try to work their way through. By 8:00 a.m. the air warmed. There was no wind and Allan Hancock was pleased to announce that it was going to be a sunny day. He hoped the sun would soften the new ice, and in the meantime he resolved to let the tide clear whatever path it would through the shifting floes.

Emmie wasn't surprised when the pain in Charley's leg returned with a vengeance. His face was a constant rictus of pain, his eyes squinted shut and his teeth bared like some wounded animal gone feral. Rivers of sweat poured down the boy's face. He cried out in agony, alternately screaming, whimpering, and moaning, filling the air with a tortured cacophony.

They pulled up to a large pan of ice and Allan climbed to its highest point to look around. All he could see, for miles around, was ice. He returned to the boat and informed the others that they would have to wait until the new ice melted before they moved.

Aaron disagreed. He wanted to start hauling the boat over the ice.

"If we start at that," Allan reasoned, "Charley won't make it."

Aaron shrugged. "It's better for him to die halfway across Hare Bay than at Maiden's Arm." Allan said nothing, so he pressed on. "If we get caught in this arm, Charley's a goner. Let's launch the boat over the ice toward Main Brook. At least we'll be near the trail leading to St. Anthony—and maybe it's all clear water inside. Then we'll go straight to Lock's Cove or Ireland's Bight, or maybe Goose Cove. It's only a short way from there to St. Anthony."

"You're right," said Allan, "but I think that after the sun gets up, around eleven o'clock, the new ice will be melted and we might get through out there." He pointed toward Goose Cove.

"You're gambling, Al. There's almost always a tide out there at the mouth of Hare Bay. If we get stuck out there or cut a hole through this punt, we're done for, but if we punch our way along the shoreline, at least we'll be able to go ashore if something goes wrong."

Allan Hancock was a reasonable man. Although he was of no relation to Fanny and her sons, he considered them family. Charley's life was at stake, and he conceded that they shouldn't take any unnecessary risks. Still, he was also a proud man.

"Mark!" he called.

"Yes?"

"Which way do you think we should go?"

Mark examined the depth of the bay, then looked toward Goose Cove, which lay nine miles away.

"Go straight to Goose Cove."

His brother Will, a steady and level-headed fellow, spoke up. "Just a minute! You're right, Aaron," he said. "Let's go in around the bay and see if it opens inside."

"Okay," said Mark, throwing up his hands, "let's go somewhere. My jingles!"

Joe Hancock had been on the move all night, accompanied by Jim Barnes, a well-known resident of the Englee–Roddickton area who spent his life around the lumber camps. They had left Englee shortly after Joe and his hot-tempered brother, Roy, returned home with no news for their mother. Joe had rounded up a dog team and headed for St. Anthony, hoping that the doctor had returned to the hospital. They were exhausted after a

THE PRICE PAID FOR CHARLEY

hard night's ride and pulled in to Lane's Pond for a few hours to give the dogs some relief. Then they pressed on toward Lock's Cove to check in with Nat Dawe, at Roy's suggestion.

First Joe checked Dr. Grenfell's cabin, but there was no sign, not even a note. He checked along the trail, but this too was a dead end. He and Jim concluded that the doctor had not even left Lock's Cove. They didn't consider the possibility that Dr. Grenfell had crossed the ice to Hare Bay—taking such a risk would have been foolhardy.

As they neared Nat Dawe's home, however, they realized that something was terribly wrong. A woman watched them from a window and came outside when they approached.

"Good day, ma'am," Joe said.

The woman nodded but said nothing. Joe Hancock was not one to mince words, so when the woman failed to respond, he turned and started walking back to the dog team.

"Excuse me, sir," the woman said, and Joe turned and faced her again. "Are you looking for someone?"

"Yes," he said flatly. He looked toward the shoreline and was surprised to see a crowd of people down there. "We're looking for Nat Dawe."

"Nat's not home. He's out on the cliffs."

"Out on the cliffs? Sealing?"

"No. He's watching for Dr. Grenfell, who drove off yesterday."

Joe could not fathom what he had just heard. He looked at Jim, who stared wide-eyed. Then Jim left the dog team and walked toward the woman. "Are you Mrs. Dawe?" he asked.

"Yes."

"Mrs. Dawe, we're from Englee. We've been on the go all night, and I can tell you that Dr. Grenfell is not around the bottom of the bay. We've checked already."

"Sir, the men saw him just before dark yesterday evening, driving out the bay on a pan of ice. Nat says that it'll be a miracle if he's ever seen again!"

"Mrs. Dawe," Joe said uneasily, "we're also searching for someone else. There are six men and a woman on a boat to St. Anthony. Do you know if anyone has seen them?"

"Oh my!" she cried. "Your boat is lost? We just sent one out to look for Dr. Grenfell!"

Joe shot a worried glance at Jim, and without a word the two men set out for the cliffs to find Nat.

22

NAT'S PUNT FINALLY STRUCK open water after being pulled through the ice by the crewmen. Each man was equipped with a "slob hauler," a pole eight feet long with a pick-shaped knob of wood at the end. They spent hours battling the angry sea and prying ice chunks apart as the small boat crept through the slob ice. Around 10:00 a.m. they reached some loose ice that opened a path leading straight to the ocean. The sun was high and the four men at the oars took off their coats. George Reid kept watch, maintaining a southerly course toward Ireland's Bight, whose residents had long since moved west for the winter. Several times the boat ran upon hidden ice and nearly capsized. The men had to be swift to push off each time the keel went aground and crunched loudly and lifted the bow skyward. After an hour or so, they encountered newer, softer ice, and their progress quickened.

"What do you think of it, Skipper?" Levi Reid asked his father.

"I'm not sure." George's cool, grey eyes fixed on the waters ahead of the craft.

"We might be looking for a dead man."

"I know, Levi."

"I haven't lost hope," said Mr. Andrews. "We'll find him, boys!"

"How far are we going to go off?" asked Levi.

"As far as the Grey Islands, maybe farther," George said, his face expressionless.

Levi looked at his brother, Bill, and shrugged.

"We must be heading in the right direction," Bill offered. "If we weren't, we would have heard a shot by now."

"We're too far out now to hear—" George began, but he was interrupted when the boat hit the ice again and the bow shot upward. He sighed. Every minute lost, Dr. Grenfell was closer to death.

The sun blazed in the heavens. Dr. Grenfell's eyes burned, and he kept them at a perpetual squint. "I'm snowblind," he croaked, his mouth and throat a searing desert. Snowblindness is a painful condition similar to that received from the flash of a bright flame.

Oh, but if only I had the materials to build a fire, he thought irrationally, casting his gaze to far-off waters and imagining all of his gear lying submerged beneath their cool depths. *A fire to warm me, and perhaps send a signal . . .* The doctor's last thought trailed off. Was it possible? It just might be. An idea came to him so quickly and filled him with so much hope

THE PRICE PAID FOR CHARLEY

that for a moment he felt he would weep, first in relief, and then in defeat.

He moved to the dog carcasses. With his knife he quickly removed the hind leg bones from all three animals and scraped off most of the clingy meat. Next he reached for the leather traces hanging from his belt. The doctor paused in mid-action and looked around at the miles and miles of ice imprisoning him. What was he thinking? It would never work; nobody could see him, and time was his enemy.

"But time is all I have now," he said, grimacing.

He gripped two of the dog bones and spliced them together, end to end, using a piece of the dogs' traces. Nodding in satisfaction, he attached another bone to the shaft, then another to the end of that bone, until all of the grisly souvenirs were connected. The doctor hefted the pole, which stretched about five feet long. He eyed his living dogs and noted they were looking at his handiwork with great interest.

"You'll get some later on," he promised.

Laying aside the pole, Dr. Grenfell took hold of his football shirt and pulled it over his head.

"How silly!" he said. "Imagine me going into the afterlife waving the Oxford Medical School standard!" He laughed despite himself as he tied the shirt's sleeves to the pole.

He raised the flag over his head and waved it. His whole body ached and cried out against the cold, his eyes and throat were burning, and his stomach rolled with nausea at the smell of the bloody dog meat that hung in chunks and tendrils from his flagpole, but the good doctor was laughing, long and hard, for the first time in what seemed like a lifetime.

No matter what she tried, Emmie could not console Charley. He was so far gone, he whimpered from the slightest touch. He cried all the time and tears fell in streams across his face. She figured that if Charley did not get to the hospital today—and maybe even if he did—the boy would die. The bone in his leg was seriously infected, and his foot was swollen badly and turning dark, a sure sign of gangrene. Emmie had no medication to offer him. His was an example of suffering at its highest level. One of the abscesses in his leg ran; the other two were large lumps inside the skin that looked ready to burst.

"What can I do?" the midwife asked in desperation as Charley groaned.

They were close to Brent Islands, and in open water. Now that they were inside the ice, they followed a lead to open water toward Goose Cove. Ahead they saw ice, and lots of it. However, the crew were not discouraged. They would have to cross Hare Bay, so they bent their backs to the oars and rowed steadily.

The men on the cliffs watched Nat's punt moving among the ice. Their guns were poised to signal, but there was no need to sound a shot. At the same time they scanned Hare Bay for any sign of Dr. Grenfell. There were eight men present, but Nat Dawe was clearly the one in charge. A haze, caused by the sun's rays, reflected off the ice, making visibility poor.

THE PRICE PAID FOR CHARLEY

Occasionally someone uttered, "I think I see something!" and the glass was quickly passed to him. But every time the alarm was raised by a mirage or the men's imaginations. Five or six miles from land, the punt disappeared from view.

Word arrived that two men wanted to talk with Nat Dawe. He went to the flat where Jim Barnes and Joe Hancock were waiting.

"I'm glad to see you two," said Nat when the introductions were made. "You're more than welcome in Lock's Cove. There's one thing that I want you to know first. It's not your fault that Dr. Grenfell is lost. We warned him not to go."

"Have you seen anyone else around the bay?" Joe asked. "Anyone besides Dr. Grenfell?"

"No, why?"

"Well, the doctor didn't arrive and my brother continued to get much worse. Two of my brothers took four more men, a woman, and Charley to St. Anthony by boat. They left yesterday morning in a twenty- two-foot open boat. They're somewhere between Englee and St. Anthony."

Nat's jaw dropped. "Did you say your name is Joe Hancock?"

"Yes."

"How sick was your brother when they left?"

"Very sick," Joe said. "We didn't think he would last the day."

"We've got a problem on our hands now with Dr. Grenfell, but it looks like yours is worse. You've got eight people in that boat. Joe, suppose your brother died before they got him to

Hare Bay. What do you think they would do? Continue on to St. Anthony or go back home?"

Joe lowered his head. "Go back home, I guess."

"But," Nat offered, "suppose he's not dead. Suppose they're still on their way—maybe crossing Hare Bay."

Jim Barnes spoke up, realizing what Nat was saying. "If they're crossing Hare Bay, they might pick up Dr. Grenfell!"

"Maybe you're right," said Nat, with a glimmer of hope in his eyes. "You know, boys, we might see a miracle yet today!"

"What do you think we should do?" Joe asked.

"There's not much you can do here. If I were you I'd go on to Goose Cove and alert the crowd there. If they come ashore here, we'll take care of them. We'll take Charley to St. Anthony and haul up the boat. The six men can walk back home, and you can pick up the woman at St. Anthony and bring her home."

Joe nodded. "Okay, that's what we'll do. Thank you."

"Listen," Nat said as an afterthought. "Go down to my house and get a lunch. Tell Lottie that I'll be home in about an hour."

The two left and Nat returned to the cliff. He told his men to watch for a white boat with eight people aboard. The new instructions brought an excited murmur to the group.

"I don't know," one man said. "Can you imagine having to row down here with a patient?"

"Yes," said Nat, "and anyone with that kind of nerve has a chance of making it. Just like Dr. Grenfell!"

Nobody spoke, but all eyes looked with renewed determination at the jungle of ice that had been carried with the current into the ocean. Fourteen individuals and eight dogs were out there somewhere, and the men watching from the cliffs above Lock's Cove resolved not to rest until every one was found.

23

GEORGE REID AND HIS crew pushed hard at the oars as a long expanse of open water appeared before them and they followed the leads, on course. They passed several seals whose necks were stretched high and whiskers quivering as they watched the curious craft. The boat leaked badly; it had taken many a beating from the ice.

"Dr. Grenfell must be near the Grey Islands by now," said Bill Reid.

Levi disagreed. "I'd say he's down with the crabs."

"Hold it, boys!" George Reid said abruptly.

The four stopped rowing.

"What is it, Skipper?" Mr. Andrews asked.

"I thought I saw something over there." George pointed to his left. "Wait until the swell comes up again."

The men looked where George had pointed, but saw nothing.

"Keep her over to the left," George warned. "We'll take a run out there."

THE PRICE PAID FOR CHARLEY

They turned the boat and followed their new course, dodging areas of ice and slob as they went. George thought he saw something again, but he only said, "Row on, boys!" He stared intently, his knuckles white as he gripped the gunwale of the boat.

"I see him, boys!" he shouted.

His words jolted the men from their concentrated efforts. They stopped rowing and sat up straight, facing the front of the boat.

"Where?" they asked, each one looking in a different direction.

"There," George said, and pointed. "I saw dogs! I'm sure of it. Right over that pan of ice. Watch, now, when the swell comes up again."

The five men looked with anxious eyes. In the distance they saw a black cluster on the ice, but it was too far away—about a mile—to identify.

"Where's Dr. Grenfell, old man?" asked Bill.

"Take it easy," George cautioned. "I've got to throw some water out of the boat, so row in that direction."

Bill nodded. "Don't lose sight of what you see, Father! Let Levi throw out the water. You keep your eyes open!"

The slob ice was soft enough to row through, and the boat got closer.

"Yes! 'Tis him, boys! He's waving a flag!"

The five crewmen stood up and just stared in awe. Dr. Grenfell was lying amid blood and fur; he was indeed waving a flag, but the men aboard the punt could tell the doctor was close to exhaustion.

"Start rowing, boys!" said George. "It's him! He's alive, boys! He's alive!"

The doctor noticed his dogs were all standing and looking in the same direction. He followed their gaze.

"I think I see something," he whispered. "Is that . . . could that be an oar?" He blinked. "Yes! And a black boat . . ." He stood with difficulty.

"It *is* a boat!" he barked. *No. No! It must be a mirage. I'm dying . . . I must be dying.* His dogs whined and beat their tails on the ice.

"Hello there!" he called weakly, his voice clawing at his throat.

There was no answer and his shoulders slumped, defeated. He gave his flag a half-hearted wave. His eyes swam from the simple strain of keeping them open.

"Brin," he said, "do you see anything?"

The dog barked excitedly.

Someone must be coming! his mind screamed.

Then a voice, the most wonderful sound the doctor had ever heard, cut through the air.

"Dr. Grenfell! It's me, George Reid! Can you hear me?"

"Dr. Grenfell, hold on!" George shouted. "Hold on! We're coming for you!"

"Don't bump the pan, boys!" Levi said. "Slow her down. We don't want to knock him into the water."

"Levi, go to the front. Slow her down! Slow her down! Put the boat side-on to the pan, boys," said George.

THE PRICE PAID FOR CHARLEY

Levi jumped to the front as the men slowed the boat and moved it parallel to the ice pan. Levi and George put their feet on the edge of the ice.

"My God!" said Mr. Andrews. He had never seen anything like this before. Here was Dr. Grenfell with barely any clothes on him. He was coated in blood and had a mutilated dog-skin draped over his shoulders. The stench from the dog carcasses was overpowering.

The five men broke down and wept, unashamed, as their doctor, their hero, struggled to stand.

"Dr. Grenfell," said George, "get aboard!"

The doctor seemed to be in a daze. Levi stepped onto the ice pan, and for a moment it looked like it was going to come apart. The dogs snarled when he took the doctor's hand.

"Come on, Dr. Grenfell!" Levi urged.

Dr. Grenfell stood up and said, "Good to see you, men."

"It's good to see you, Dr. Grenfell," George replied.

The men put their arms around him and helped him into the punt. They seated him in the stern and placed a blanket over him.

"Is there anything else you want, Doctor?" asked Mr. Andrews.

"Yes. Please take my dogs aboard. And one more thing."

"What's that?"

"I want you to take those dog-skins and my flagpole."

Mr. Andrews looked at the bloody pelts on the ice pan. He couldn't for the life of him figure why the doctor would want to be reminded of his near-death experience.

"So I can show the people what happened here," Dr. Grenfell said, as if in answer to his unasked question.

"We've got no business here! We should've gone straight through outside!" Aaron Reid was mad. He and his crewmates had been hauling their boat for hours over ice and slob. Now they were in the middle of Hare Bay and making little headway. "If the wind picks up, we'll be here for a month! Trouble, trouble, trouble, that's all I've seen!

"Head her for Goose Cove!" he snapped. "If we can get there, you can take Charley to St. Anthony by dogsled. It's only ten miles. I'll tell you one thing: once I get my feet on solid ground, I'll be heading for Englee!"

Mark grinned. "You won't be heading for Englee, Aaron. You haven't got any snowshoes."

Aaron glared at him. "Mark," he said in a quiet voice, "snowshoes or not, *Aaron Reid* is going home."

"I'm well aware of that," said Mark, "but there's no need to get mad. I don't want you kicking out the side of the boat."

Nat Dawe steadied his arm on a nearby rock and looked through the spyglass. He drew in a sharp breath.

"I see a boat!"

The other men scrambled around him.

"Where? Show us!"

Nat stared in a southwesterly direction. "I see a boat, all right—and she's mine!"

He offered the glass to one of the other men. When they all

grabbed for it at once, he said, "One at a time! Boys, if you drop that glass, George will have my head. Now, listen. I'm going back to tell the others that George is on his way in. I should be back in an hour or so."

When he returned, his men turned to him at once.

"We see the boat!" they cried. "Look! You can see her without the glass now!"

Nat went directly to the man with the spyglass. "What do you see?"

The man handed him the instrument. "I could only see five men, but there's something in the front of the boat. I'm not sure what it is."

"Dogs," Nat said slowly, peering through the glass. "But I don't see Dr. Grenfell. The boys are pulling on the oars for dear life! Wait . . . that's Dr. Grenfell's dogs!"

He looked up and saw that everyone from town, young and old alike, was coming to the shoreline. Women carried babies in their arms. Loose dogs ran along the surf. Children ran screaming to the water's edge. A lump rose in Nat's throat at the sight. He looked through the glass again; the boat was less than a mile from Lock's Cove.

"They've got him! There's no mistake! They have him on board!"

24

THE WHOLE TOWN OF Lock's Cove watched as Nat Dawe's black punt rounded the point of land and raced toward the harbour. A great cheer erupted from the shore when they saw that the blanket-wrapped figure on board was Dr. Grenfell. Immediately a few men launched a small rowboat to meet George Reid and the others, whose boat was struggling through ice and against the tide. Some men on the shore fed the rowers a line of rope. They kept tying on additional pieces when the line grew taut. When the rowboat reached the punt, the men attached the line to it. Thus conjoined, they signalled the townspeople onshore, who pulled the two boats to safety in the space of ten minutes.

Dr. Grenfell shivered beneath his blanket. The people crowding around the punt just stared in disbelief. He looked like an old man of the sea, wasted, half-dead, and caked with dried blood they hoped was not his. They looked at him for several long moments, tears flowing freely down their faces.

Finally, the doctor asked if someone would help him stand.

THE PRICE PAID FOR CHARLEY

He looked around him at the tear-streaked faces and the relief evident in each one. These were Newfoundlanders and they loved him to a fault. The English doctor had never before felt like he belonged as much as he did at that moment.

George Reid and Levi Dawe helped him out of the boat.

"Thank you," Dr. Grenfell said. "I think I can make it on my own now."

"Are you sure, Doctor?" Levi asked, throwing George a worried glance.

"Let me try."

They let him go. He made several faltering steps, and they grabbed him.

"It's that rolling out there," he explained.

"Come on, Doctor," said George. "Let's go to the house."

When they went inside, Aunt Rachel Reid walked up to Dr. Grenfell. She cried and covered her face with her hands.

"My, oh my, Doctor!" she said. "What a miracle! I've got the bed ready, George. Bring him in."

"George," the doctor said when the old gentleman took him by the arm.

"Yes?"

"Get your dog team ready. We're leaving right away for St. Anthony."

The colour drained from George's face.

"Doctor, you can't even walk!"

"I know. I'm going to ride. And George, make sure that you take everything you brought in. The flagpole and the dog carcasses. Everything! Put it in a coach box."

"Okay, Doctor. Bill," he said, turning to his son, "get the dog team ready for St. Anthony, and get the two coach boxes ready."

"I'll do that," Nat volunteered. "Bill, you go on in the house and get some rest."

Before they said their goodbyes, the men who had commandeered the punt stood around Dr. Grenfell when he motioned for them to come near.

"Gentlemen," he said, "I will be rewarding you for what you've done for me."

George shook his head. "Dr. Grenfell, you don't owe us anything. In fact, we owe you something."

"What would that be?"

"Our lives."

Dr. Grenfell wept then. He held out one of his swollen hands and gave each man a hearty handshake.

"I love every one of you," he said.

Joe Hancock and Jim Barnes stood high on the cliffs at the headlands between Ireland's Bight and Goose Cove while their dogs lay curled up on the soft, sun-warmed caribou moss nearby. The sun blasted the icefield 400 feet below them, making the sea look like a shimmering white carpet. They talked about life on the Great Northern Peninsula. All winter it had seemed impossible to work in the lumber woods. All they did was attend funerals or go back and forth to St. Anthony for doctors. It seemed that everybody was crying over someone dying.

THE PRICE PAID FOR CHARLEY

"Look, Joe," said Jim. "A boat!"

"Where?"

"Out there!" Jim said, and pointed.

"I see it!" Joe exclaimed. "It's black . . . Nat said the boat they sent to look for Dr. Grenfell was black."

"That's it, Joe! For sure! I wonder if they found him?"

"They must have found something, or they wouldn't be returning. At least for a couple of hours yet." Joe sighed. "Or maybe the ice out there was too tight for them to move."

They watched the black boat for an hour, until it disappeared behind one of the cliffs near Lock's Cove. The sun began to dip in the west as the pair scanned every open lead of water and piece of ice in Hare Bay.

"I think I see something!" Joe said. He squinted against the lowering sun.

"Where, Joe?"

"Right out there!"

Jim opened his mouth to speak, but then he saw it too. "I see it!" he said. "It's a white boat!"

"There's an open lead right ahead," said Joe. "If only we could talk to them."

"I wonder how poor Charley is," Jim remarked. "He must be alive, because they're still heading toward St. Anthony."

"If the crowd from Lock's Cove found Dr. Grenfell, then Charley came pretty close to meeting the doctor out in the middle of Hare Bay." Joe laughed. "Wouldn't that have been something! But I'd say that Dr. Grenfell's bones have been picked clean by now."

"It's in the lead now, and they have open water all the way to Goose Cove," Jim observed as the boat came closer.

"They'll be in St. Anthony tonight," Joe said. "Let's go!"

Jim nodded, and the two men left the cliffside.

The news of the loss of Dr. Grenfell had reached St. Anthony. People cried or wandered vacant-eyed, occasionally casting fearful glances to the western trail as the news spread around town. Every time the story was told, pieces were added to the tale, each addition making the story worse.

As the first dog came into view late that evening, there was a stir among the townspeople. "He's coming!" someone shouted, and people rushed out of the hospital to see if the doctor was alive—or if the dog team were carrying his corpse. Then all three dog teams were in view. The smell of woodsmoke from stovepipes and the questioning howls from an unseen dog set the stage for Dr. Grenfell as his team pulled up to the hospital's entrance. Team drivers yelled and dog whips cracked, and at last, the sound of cheering rose into the darkening sky as the English doctor made his entrance. Some pushed to get nearer, but they were restrained by Wilfred Elliot and Walter Short of Lock's Cove, who had hauled Dr. Grenfell and his things to St. Anthony.

Dr. Little met Dr. Grenfell and helped him from the coach box. The trip from Lock's Cove had been a rough one; he could hardly stand.

"Get the stretcher!" commanded a nurse.

"No," said Dr. Grenfell, "I'll make it on my own."

THE PRICE PAID FOR CHARLEY

Now standing, he revealed his garments: a sealskin vest he had put together, and the puttees, wrapped around his legs, stuffed with oakum. His eyes were red and swollen from snow-blindness, he limped noticeably, and bits of blood and gore still clung to him.

"Reuben, take all my things to the dog-shed, and make sure that nothing is removed. I will have a word with you as soon as I can."

Reuben Simms, the doctor's dog team driver, nodded. "Yes, Doctor," he said, and left.

Dr. Grenfell was led into the hospital. "Thank God I'm back! Someone please draw me a bath."

"Not until we have a look at you first," Dr. Little said. After they escorted him to the emergency ward, he said, "What an awful odour on you, Wilfred!"

"Yes," Dr. Grenfell admitted, "and it's what saved my life, John."

Dr. Little gave him a shot of morphine. "This will help you," he said.

"Has anyone heard from Charley Hancock?" Dr. Grenfell inquired.

"No, not yet, sir," responded Dr. Little. "But you're going to be all right."

Emmie bent over Charley, expecting the worst. His lips were purple and his eyes were closed. At times his arms shook; he appeared to be having convulsions. There was nothing she could do for him. *At least he's unconscious*, she thought.

The boat sped along as the oarsmen gave their all. Emmie realized they had been travelling ice-free for some time. She had not heard Aaron screaming at the ice in awhile, so she figured things were okay.

Suppose Dr. Grenfell arrived at Englee and discovered that Charley had gone by boat to St. Anthony. What will he say? Will he be mad?

"How far are we now, Aaron?" she called.

"We're almost at the entrance to Goose Cove. It looks like open water all the way in to the harbour! We should be there in an hour."

"Why are you going into the harbour, Aaron?"

Aaron was no weakling, nor was he scared of anything. Now, however, he had to search for an answer to Emmie's question, because the men planned to end their boat trip at Goose Cove and take Charley the last ten miles to St. Anthony on dogsled.

"We're going to check on the ice," he explained, "to ask someone about the ice conditions." He knew he couldn't fool Emmie for long.

"Aaron," she said sternly, "what have you got planned?"

"Look, Emmie," he said, poking his head through the small doorway, "it looks like a solid jam of ice out near Goose Cove. It might be close to the land all the way to St. Anthony. "

"Maybe," Emmie admitted, "but I say we should go on. I'll tell you one thing: Charley isn't going to be taken out of this boat until he gets to St. Anthony, so if he has to be hauled there from Goose Cove, they'll have to haul this boat too!"

THE PRICE PAID FOR CHARLEY

Aaron went to Allan Hancock, who was in charge, and told him what Emmie had said.

"No problem," Allan said. "Keep her off, boys! We're heading for St. Anthony, even if we have to spend the rest of the spring in The Oven!" Halfway between Goose Cove and St. Anthony is a place the fishermen called "The Oven," a large cave that extends into the shear rock at the base of a 500-foot cliff. Its opening is small but the cave is considerably large inside and even contains a sandy beach. In June, schools of capelin would go to the subterranean beach to lay their spawn eggs.

Long after dark the skiff passed The Oven and moved quickly along the rocky coast, hugging the shoreline a few feet outside the breaking waves. It was a nerve-racking experience, but each man held his ground.

"Are there any shoals around here?" Mark asked.

"We'll know if we strike one," Aaron grumbled.

The ice appeared to be tight to the shoreline, but far enough off the land for them to slip by. They forced the boat onward in silence. At midnight they passed the lighthouse on Fishing Point at the three-mile entrance to St. Anthony. An hour later the white boat from Englee pulled in to the St. Anthony wharf. The crew were surprised to see two nurses waiting for them, along with Joe Hancock and Jim Barnes.

Mark and the others pulled their boat up on the ice and helped Emmie out. She informed the nurses that Charley was in bad shape and had to be handled gently. Nodding, the nurses placed him on a stretcher and carried him to the hospital, accompanied by the Hancock brothers and the rest of the crew that had braved the frigid northern waters. Jim Barnes and Joe Hancock fell in beside Emmie as they walked and told her of Dr. Grenfell's harrowing experience on the ice and his daring rescue. She was speechless.

When they reached the hospital, Mark, Aaron, Allan, and the others stood to one side as Dr. Little examined Charley. He found that the infected leg would require surgery as soon as possible. However, he regretted to inform Charley's brothers that the boy was terribly undernourished and would likely die if he underwent surgery at this time. Instead, the doctor opened the infected area to allow it to drain. This, he said, should buy Charley some time.

The Hancock brothers sent word to Englee that Charley had survived the trip. They waited for their mother to arrive and decided they would stay in St. Anthony until Charley's condition improved . . . or if he took a turn for the worse.

Epilogue

OVER THE NEXT FEW weeks, the doctors at the St. Anthony hospital fed Charley vitamins to build up his stamina. Dr. Grenfell himself dropped by to visit Charley from time to time. They quickly became friends, and during his visits the doctor would regale the boy with stories of the many adventures he'd had in Newfoundland. His most recent escapade, of course, was the most popular story floating around town, but he also told Charley of his initial trip to the colony and how the first sight that greeted him upon his arrival was the capital city, St. John's, engulfed in flames. He went on to describe a tragic case involving a young woman who had hid the shame of her pregnancy until it was too late. All of these stories and more Charley listened to with fascination, all the while feeling honoured that this great doctor elected to spend so much time with him.

By May 25 of that year, Charley was deemed fit for surgery. Dr. Little performed the operation, which was a success. Of course Charley's good friend Dr. Grenfell visited him while he recuperated, and Charley and his family expressed endless gratitude. Fanny Hancock and her sons were elated when the doctor told them that he expected Charley would be well enough to go home in August.

When August came and the Hancock family readied their dog team for the long trip back to Englee, Dr. Grenfell met them in front of the hospital and embraced them one by one. He waved as they left, his gaze lingering for some time on the proud dogs that made up the Hancocks' team, then turned back toward the hospital.

Afterword

A couple of days after Dr. Grenfell was rescued, he took all the items he had had with him on the ice pan, including his five remaining dogs, to a remote spot at the back of the hospital. Dressed in the same outfit he had worn while adrift in Hare Bay, he stood in the snowdrifts with his dog-bone flagpole and posed for a photograph. His press secretary sent his report, including the picture, to the major newspapers of the world. As a result donations poured in to help him with his work, and he was invited to lecture through Europe and across North America.

Dr. Grenfell recorded that in 1912 he hired a Samuel Pilgrim of St. Lunaire–Griquet—and that he was the main cause of the reindeer project's failure. At one point Samuel persuaded his poacher friends to go to the bottom of Hare Bay, where he drove the caribou across the imaginary line. The government had advised Dr. Grenfell that, if any of his reindeer were found to the west of this line, they could be shot as native caribou. Samuel Pilgrim and his friends opened fire on the animals with rifles and shotguns, killing 250 of them in less than ten minutes.

Thomas Boyd of Main Brook fondly remembers, and speaks highly of, Dr. Grenfell and his humanitarian work in Newfoundland and Labrador. Thomas was born in St. Anthony. As a boy he often saw the doctor when he went with his father to Main Brook each spring for a week's vacation. The eight-year-old was present at the sod-turning ceremony for Dr. Grenfell's hospital at St. Anthony, and witnessed the laying of its foundation in 1903.

"We youngsters," Thomas reminisces, "were around Dr. Grenfell all the time. People young and old were his product. He started a school there, too, and I got my education. In 1912, when I was seventeen, I was sent to Baie Verte to learn telegraphy."

One morning after readying the set, Thomas heard a message coming through. Putting on his headphones, he started writing furiously: "The *Titanic* has struck an iceberg, and is going down." The date was April 15, 1912.

Thomas returned to St. Anthony late that summer and set up a wireless station. His first message was, "Station set up. Everything working okay." Dr. Grenfell wanted all of the days' news delivered to him at his office. Thomas objected, and this resulted in an argument. However, Thomas stood his ground.

Thomas Boyd recalls the story of an airplane that flew over St. Anthony one day when he was a young man. "I think it was the first one we had ever seen," he remembers. "We heard talk of airplanes and had read about them, but none ever came our way. Around noon we heard a loud noise. It was March month."

THE PRICE PAID FOR CHARLEY

The plane circled high above the hospital and, in just a few moments, everyone in St. Anthony crowded the shoreline. It circled back, cleared the town, and came over the harbour. The side door opened and something was thrown out. A parachute opened as it fell, and everyone rushed to the object when it landed. To their surprise it turned out to be a large husky dog. The tag was addressed "To Dr. Grenfell, from Admiral Peary." The plane circled three times, and three more dogs were thrown out. Circling over the hospital one more time, it levelled its wing and left.

Apparently the four dogs were members of Captain Bob Bartlett's team, the one he used when he went with Admiral Robert Edwin Peary (1856–1920) on his famous expedition to the North Pole. "I don't know about that," Thomas laughs, "but I was there when the dogs fell from the heavens. They were sled dogs, worth a dozen like the ones that Dr. Grenfell had killed on the ice."

"Lady Grenfell," continues Thomas, "had a private seamstress, Nellie Taylor, from Raleigh. I began going with her, and later married her. Lady Grenfell came from a rich family in the States. They had two sons, Wilfred and Pascoe, and one daughter, Rosamund. Nellie made all their clothes, and most everything for those at the Mission."

One day Nellie delivered a roll of cloth to Dr. Grenfell's residence.

"Come in," the doctor invited Nellie. "Here's a job for you, my dear."

"Yes, Doctor, what is it?" she asked.

"A very close friend of mine is going on an expedition. Admiral Byrd, his name is. He is going to the Antarctic. He is a flyer, and I want you to make him a full suit of Arctic clothing out of this Grenfell cloth, of course. He will be coming this way soon to pick up men and dogs for his expedition. I want this made, and all ready for him, within a month."

Nellie had the clothes ready on time. When Admiral Richard E. Byrd (1888–1957) stopped over, Thomas Boyd's first cousin, Jacob Bussey (later changed to Bursey) of St. Lunaire, White Bay, went with Byrd on his journey to the South Pole.

One day, Thomas recalls, a Navy ship entered St. Anthony's harbour. The ship anchored offshore, and the Governor stepped on land. The Guard of Honour, and many spectators, walked toward the hospital. The doors opened, and Dr. Grenfell and his staff emerged. As they approached the Guard of Honour, the Governor drew his sword and advanced toward Dr. Grenfell. Halting before him, he said in a booming voice, "Dr. Wilfred Grenfell, in the name of His Majesty the King, I bestow on you the order of St. George." He placed the sword across Dr. Grenfell's shoulder. The doctor had been knighted and was now Sir Wilfred T. Grenfell.

* * *

At home with a cup of tea near his elbow, Dr. Baxter T. Gillard smiled as he completed telling me the story of Dr. Grenfell's ordeal on the ice. I asked him what he thought of the doctor in summary.

"To tell the truth," he said, "it's a job to sum up in just a few words, to give the true picture of Dr. Grenfell. He was our chairman on the village council here at Englee, on which I served with him. We had great times and rough times, but I think the greatest thing that Dr. Grenfell had was a heart of gold. I think that if one has that, then everything else will follow."

Dr. Gillard then told me about Charley Hancock.

"The boy was always sick, and he continued to hobble and limp around Englee for years after his operation. He went back and forth to St. Anthony for a couple of years. A short while after Dr. Grenfell went adrift, Charley took sick again. I was fourteen at the time. I remember it quite well.

"I came out of Sunday school at four o'clock. As I left the church, Reverend Tiller said, 'Baxter, I'm going up to Aunt Fanny Hancock's to pray with poor Charley. Would you like to come along?'

"'Yes, sir,' I replied, 'I certainly would.'

"The two of us went along. Aunt Fanny welcomed us, and was glad to see us. When we entered the house, we saw Charley laying on the couch with a white pillow under his head. He was the picture of death. Reverend Tiller went over to where he was laying and said, 'How are you doing, Charley?'

"Charley nodded his head.

"'Can you hear me?' the reverend asked.

"Charley indicated that he could.

"'Are you saved, Charley?'

"Charley nodded again. That's when he started coughing. He turned red, then black.

"'I think Charley is going to throw up, Mrs. Hancock,' Reverend Tiller said.

"Aunt Fanny ran in with a large white pan and placed it on the floor near Charley. She put a hand on his forehead, and another on his chest, and held Charley over the pan. It seemed that his lungs gave out. He threw up, then went limp. She turned him over onto his back and put his head on the pillow. One look at him and I didn't need anyone to tell me that Charley Hancock was dead.

"'Oh my!' said Fanny. 'Charley has fainted! Someone go for Aunt Lizzie!'

"The reverend spoke up. 'It's too late, Aunt Fanny . . . Charley is dead.'

"She sat down in a rocking chair without a word and put her apron to her eyes. She cried softly as Reverend Tiller opened his Bible and began to read aloud. I stayed with them for a while and prayed, and I couldn't hold back my own tears for poor Charley Hancock."

Stories from the
Great Northern Peninsula

Job Gillard tells a story about the harsh winter conditions on the Great Northern Peninsula.

"I was asked one day in March to take a maternity patient from Englee to St. Anthony. I naturally accepted—I've never turned down anyone in my life. I had a good team of twelve dogs, so I asked Giddon 'Gead' Lane to go with me. We picked up the woman and put her in a coach box. We left at 7:00 a.m. on Sunday, and arrived in St. Anthony at 5:00 p.m. The going was pretty good.

"At seven o'clock we went to a meeting at the Salvation Army. While there we received word that Myrtle Lane, Gead Lane's sister, was ready to go home. She had been a patient at the hospital for a month. I was asked to take her, and again, I agreed. We told the messenger that we'd be leaving between 6:00 and 7:00 a.m., so they were to have her ready.

"We had a glorious time at the meeting, and while leaving I shook hands with a Mr. Wesley Pilgrim. He told me that we were going to have a big northeaster, and that we could be in for a couple of days of bad weather. We stayed with him and got up at five o'clock and went outside. It was cloudy and a storm was in the air. I knew that if I could get over the White Hills I could brave a bad storm around Hare Bay, because a line had been cut most of the way.

"At six o'clock we went to the annex and got Myrtle, tucked her in the coach box, and started out. It was just getting daylight, and a little snow was falling. I said to Gead, 'The storm is coming!' The dogs knew they were heading home, and they were crazy to leave. I knew the route; I had made twenty-seven trips there."

Of the twenty-seven trips he had made, Job had only been paid for one! George Hall, manager of the Roddickton Saunders and Howell Lumber Company, had given him fifteen dollars. Job had transported George's sister Emmie, who was extremely sick. Job didn't charge anything, but he was given the money when he returned. In those days money was hard to come by and was gratefully received.

"Anyway, when I got up on the White Hills," Job continues, "the weather thickened. It was hard going underfoot, but Gead and I didn't have to wear snowshoes. When we got to Ireland's Bight Valley, the weather lightened a little. I picked up some speed. I got on the komatik again, but when we got to Three Brook Ponds, the weather got worse. We kept inside Lock's Cove. A storm came on, the worst I have ever seen! I managed to get ahead. It took us three hours to go three miles.

"We finally got to the bottom of Hare Bay. By now I had to wear my snowshoes. We were in a hurricane! At 1:00 p.m. we arrived at Main Brook and went to Dr. Grenfell's cabin at Southwest Pond. We got Myrtle into the cabin. We got the fire going and the cabin warmed, but she was still shivering. I boiled the water and gave her hot tea. Then she felt pretty good.

THE PRICE PAID FOR CHARLEY

"'We're over the worst of it,' I told them. 'It's mostly woods now, so we'll move on.'

"They agreed and we pushed on, with me walking ahead. It was dark when we reached the bottom of Canada Bay, three miles from Roddickton. A couple of families, including Uncle John Carroll's, lived there. Uncle John wanted us to stay, but I said that if we came this far we would continue. So we did. As we came along the shoreline, I wandered into the trees, and we had quite a time trying to get out! We came along to the area of Camp Cove. I called to Gead to stop the team.

"'What's the matter, Job?' he asked.

"'I can smell smoke!'

"I told him to wait a moment while I looked around. Immediately I got smoke in my eyes. I reached out my hands and felt something metal.

"I called back to Gead, 'We're on the roof of someone's house. This is the stovepipe!'"

Henry O'Neill was from Carrick-on-Suir, a small town located near the border of Tipperary and Waterford County, Ireland. In 1845 he and his sister, whose parents had died, left their native country, like many of their young countrymen. The potato famine was at its worst; the plague had taken four million lives in the space of a few years.

The O'Neills went to Liverpool, England, where Henry secured a job on a ship sailing on foreign voyages. Late one fall he was shipwrecked in the Strait of Belle Isle, at the top of the Great Northern Peninsula, Newfoundland. History records that he built a small house from sticks, sods, and stones, probably on Quirpon Island, and spent the winter there.

In early spring he started walking south, following the shoreline. It is likely that he crossed Hare Bay, close to where Dr. Grenfell fell through the ice half a century later. Early in April he arrived at the small town of Conche and met a John Casey, who had arrived there from St. John's a year earlier and lived in an abandoned French fishing room.

Henry told his life story to John. When the former mentioned the name of his hometown, he was received with open arms. As it turned out, John's wife, Mary, hailed from Waterford County. With this welcome Henry moved into John's home, ending his roving days. In less than a year he married John Casey's daughter, whose name was also Mary.

Henry soon put together a dog team. In those days the animals were hard to obtain. He secured them as puppies and raised them, and by his second winter in Conche, he had a strong team. Like Dr. Grenfell he was a great lover of the animals.

In March every year seal herds come south and have their young on the ice floes. Many times they pup near the coast of the Great Northern Peninsula, and the landsmen would go on the pack ice to hunt them. The people of Conche have for over a hundred years been taking part in the seal harvest. Henry O'Neill quickly became an excellent sealer.

THE PRICE PAID FOR CHARLEY

In the fall of 1852, a son was born to Henry and Mary O'Neill. He was named John after his grandfather, John Casey. The parents were happy, although times were rough around the coast. The hard-working Henry, however, provided a good living for his young family.

Early in March 1853 huge sheets of ice from the north were carried south by the Arctic current, grinding and swirling their way along the Labrador coast and pushing and smashing anything in their path. This is the type of ice that the female harp seals follow. The ice arrived in the Conche area and lodged against the shore.

On Wednesday, March 9, Henry and John went with their dogs to the icefields, where they had a successful day. The next day before the sun rose, they moved out to Shoal Point, which is located near the entrance to Crouse Harbour. It was a beautiful, but cool, morning. Henry encouraged his young, sprightly dogs to move faster. His father-in-law sat on a box at the rear of the komatik.

As the sun crested the hills to the east, they reached Shoal Point. Hitching their dogs and komatik to a small tree, they climbed a cliff to survey the ice. The majestic splendour that lay before them was breathtaking. The sun cast its glow along the mighty field of pack ice, and the different colours reflected in the glittering floes would make any person stop for a moment to view nature at its best.

Other people arrived and attention was again focused on the seal hunt. Henry and John moved onto the ice with their dog team, while the others left theirs onshore. The morning warmed and by midday not a cloud had appeared in the sky. The sealers were in a cheerful mood, anticipating a successful harvest. Henry and John moved offshore two miles and travelled east another mile or so. The going was too rough for their komatik to be pulled any farther, so they tied their dogs to a piece of ice they walked out farther, killing young seals as they went, and hauling them back to the sled.

Late in the afternoon dark clouds suddenly appeared in the western sky. At first the men paid them no mind, but when the air suddenly stirred with a gust of wind, every sealer started yelling.

"Everyone get ashore as quickly as possible!"

The hunters scurried toward Shoal Point. Soon the sky turned black and the sun retreated. A vicious wind began to blow.

"John," said Henry, "you run for Shoal Point. I'm going for the dogs. I can't leave them."

"Forget the dogs, Henry! They might make it in themselves."

"No, I can't. You go on."

John knew it was futile to argue with the Irishman. He knew how much Henry loved his dogs.

"Okay," said John, "but hurry!"

"I will," Henry shouted as he left.

Visibility decreased as more and more snow began to fall. Everyone but John and Henry made it to safety on land. John stayed on the ice near the shore while his fellow hunters begged him to come ashore.

THE PRICE PAID FOR CHARLEY

"I can't!" he cried. "I can't leave Henry."

The men on the cliffs watched as Henry reached his dogs and started toward Shoal Point. The ice started moving off from shore.

"Jump to shore, John!" they cried in unison.

A look of agony crossed John's face as he stared alternately toward the icefield, the ocean, and the swirling snowdrifts that were stirred by the northwest gales.

"I can't!" he repeated, looking at the shoreline. "I can't leave Henry to die. He's the best friend I've ever known!"

"Jump! Jump to shore! It's your last chance!"

The ice moved out slowly, three, four, five, six, then seven feet. A rope was thrown and it landed near John's feet. Instead he turned and ran for the area where Henry had gone for his dogs. Those on the cliffs saw the two men meet and redirect the dog team toward Northeast Crouse Head. Suddenly the force of the blizzard struck, and a wall of snow shut them from view. It was the last time Henry O'Neill and John Casey were seen.

That night the two widows, mother and daughter, huddled around the wood stove praying that John and Henry would be found alive. A five-month-old infant slept soundly in his cot. The wind howled and roared, as if trying to dismantle the house.

Early the next morning the wind subsided. The sun came up and shone with a sparkling brilliance across the mighty deep. The men of Conche went out in boats and sought the missing duo. For days they continued the search, but not a trace of them was ever found. They had either blown into the water or had lost their lives to the crunching ice.

A mysterious occurrence is connected with this story. One night the following September, the two women were eating supper, still grieving the loss of their loved ones. They heard scratching at the door. One of them quickly went to the door and opened it. Standing before her was one of Henry O'Neill's dogs, one that had been on the ice with the men on that fateful day.

The winter of 1934 was a stormy one on the Great Northern Peninsula. The weather was so severe that only the toughest of people dared to travel. To be outside was near-suicidal. One day in January the wind had blown northwest for twenty-four hours, with no sign of letting up. The small houses in Main Brook huddled close to the ground among the trees.

"I hear something," said Ron Ollerhead. He scanned the windowpane, but he couldn't see a thing through the thick frost.

"So do I," said Charley Pilgrim, who sat at the kitchen table. He jumped to his feet, catlike.

Charley Pilgrim was no ordinary man. He had been born and reared in Griquet, a little community on the tip of the Great Northern Peninsula. He could leap over fences at will; he was active as a young boy and was known around the area as an energetic fellow who was always on the move. Fishing with

THE PRICE PAID FOR CHARLEY

his father from an early age, this life proved to be too dull for young Charley, so at sixteen years of age, he decided to leave home. He went to St. Anthony, which was twenty miles away, and signed on as a crew member aboard a three-masted square-rigger. The boat hauled dried codfish from Newfoundland to the United States and the Caribbean. This was the life for Charley Pilgrim.

After a year on the briny ocean, his boat was wrecked somewhere along the shoreline of Long Island, near New York. Charley soon moved to New York City. After he secured a job, he began to enjoy living in the big city. However, needing more excitement, he decided to join a boxing club and try the sport. He had all the makings of an athlete and soon showed potential as a professional boxer. But this was not to be, because Charley had a problem: he had been born on the edge of the ocean. The part of his nature that sometimes will not allow one to control his own destiny got the better of him. He could not remain in New York City to become a boxer. Eventually he returned to his hometown and became a fisherman. He fished for cod in the summer and worked in the lumber woods at Roddickton in the winter.

On this day in January, Charley Pilgrim was trying to get back home to Griquet. He had come to Main Brook the day before to relay the news to his uncle Sam that his seven-year-old granddaughter had died. Of course, due to the raging blizzard, he had been held up at Ronald Ollerhead's home.

Charley, dressed in his shirt sleeves, went to investigate the sound at the door.

The man at the door was the famous Job Gillard, who was known in the days of dog team travel for his charity work of hauling sick people to and from the St. Anthony hospital. Job was returning to Roddickton after having taken a patient to St. Anthony.

"Job," said Charley, "did you come across the bay?"

"Yes, I did, Charley," Job answered as he stepped inside the house and shut the door. "What a storm! I think I could say that I blew across the bay!" He grinned. "I never saw a thing from the time I left the cliffs on the other side of the bay till I got here to the house."

"You're just in time for something to eat, Job," said Ron.

Job thanked him.

"A bad storm," Ron commented as he stood.

"You'd better believe it!" said Job. "I was lucky I had the wind at my back. But the wind's not the biggest problem. 'Tis the cold. The dogs can hardly run! 'Tis like they're all freezing. I don't think I've ever seen it so cold. 'Tis enough to cut the skin right off you."

"'Tis no time to be out," agreed Ron.

"I'm going on as soon as I get something to eat," said Job.

Charley looked up. "Are you?"

"Yes, I am. It should be pretty good from here to Roddickton because it's mostly woods."

Job sat at the table and told Ron all the news from the area as he ate. Then, as quickly as he had arrived, he was gone, disappearing into the blizzard.

Charley sat near the stove for a few minutes after Job left.

THE PRICE PAID FOR CHARLEY

"It looks to me like there's a dally in the wind," he said, referring to a break or delay in the weather.

"I don't know about that," said Ron.

"If Job Gillard can leave St. Anthony and go all the way through to Roddickton," Charley argued, "then I should be able to go home to Griquet."

"I don't know about that," Ron cautioned. "You just take a look at the weather glass. It's bottom-up."

"I think I can do it."

"Listen, Charley," Ron continued, "Job had the wind at his back. You'll have the full force of the wind in your face."

Charley thought for a moment. "Job just came across," he reasoned. "All I have to do is put the dogs on his tracks, then lay down on the komatik. The animals will pull me right across the bay! The leader is *sure* to stay on his tracks."

"I don't want you to go, Charley."

Charley said nothing as he prepared to leave.

By 1:00 p.m. Charley had his dogs harnessed and ready to leave. Hardly a thing could be seen. Ron begged him again not to go, but Charley wanted to get home and refused to listen. His eight dogs strained to dash ahead, barking wildly and tugging at their traces. Thanking Ron and the Ollerhead family for their kindness, Charley Pilgrim said goodbye and, in a few minutes, vanished into the storm.

Charley's lead dog, which had made the trip many times before, was skilled and obedient. He knew the animal would not leave the trail, no matter what. As he had planned, Charley lay face down on the komatik and didn't bother to look up.

Almost four miles into his journey, he felt the komatik strike something. The sled almost capsized and the dog team slowed down considerably. He called for the animals to stop, and they obeyed. Looking around he observed that he was near the shoreline of Brent Islands. Knowing he was on the right track, he gave a sigh of relief.

"Good dogs!" he said as they came around him. Their eagerness had disappeared. Some whined, some lifted their paws as if in supplication, some shook their heads. Charley immediately realized the problem: the animals' paws and ears were freezing. But what could he do? There was no choice but to go on. He knew that if he could get across the bay and in the shelter of the cliffs, he would not have as much trouble reaching Ireland's Bight. The dogs were almost stiff from the cold, so he had to move as quickly as possible. He again lay flat on the komatik.

"Okay, Black," he called. "Move her out!"

The lead dog moved into action, and the rest of the team took up the chase in Job Gillard's tracks.

After a half-hour or so, the dog team stopped. Sheltering his face from the piercing wind with his hand, Charley guided himself with his other hand to the nose of the komatik. He spied something in the snow and bent down to take a closer look. It was one of his dogs. He caught the animal by its harness, but he was surprised to find that the dog was dead! It had frozen to death. He called the others. Only five answered his call, and they were not faring well.

Charley took a moment to survey his surroundings. He had

THE PRICE PAID FOR CHARLEY

no compass, so he could not get his bearings. All he knew was that he was somewhere in Hare Bay. He hoped he was still on Job Gillard's tracks. The wind was still in his face, but he took no comfort in that; for all he knew it might have changed direction.

"Okay, dogs," he shouted above the howling wind. Cutting the traces from the dead dogs with his axe, he ordered the remaining team members to get moving.

It seemed like an eternity before Charley reached the base of the cliffs between Ireland's Bight and Lock's Cove. His feet felt like blocks of ice, and he had a severe pain in his back. It was a struggle to move at all. He stood and looked at the solid granite cliffs nearby and the raging storm around him. Darkness would fall soon and he would be in deep trouble. He had to get himself and his dogs into a shelter, or else they would all die. But where? He knew he could not get to Ireland's Bight, which was still four miles away. Nor would he be able to get to Lock's Cove, which was three miles distant. He would have to find shelter in the immediate area if he hoped to survive.

Glancing around he saw a large snowdrift close to the cliff. *My only hope*, he thought, *is to dig in.* Moving quickly to the drift, he started to chop the hard snow with his axe. The snow swirled around and stuck to his face. He continued chopping until he went through the hard crust, which was almost six inches thick. He then started to scoop out a hole while his dog team remained close by. It was dark by the time Charley had dug a hole large enough to fit them all. He put his dogs into the pit and placed the komatik near the hole. Next he crawled inside, dragged the sled over the hole, and stuck some hard snow over the entrance.

Charley's father had always told him, "If you're to survive in this world, you'll have to work hard." As he sat in the semi-darkness with the five dogs around him, he knew that his survival depended entirely on his animals. The small shelter would keep out the wind, but not the chill from the bitter cold. He squirmed until half of his body was in the snow. Laying on the floor of his makeshift snow-house, he got his dogs to lay around him and on top of him.

To tell the complete story of Charley Pilgrim and what he suffered during the three days and nights on the ice and around the shoreline of Hare Bay would take a full-length book. Suffice to say that the ordeal caused Charley to go to an early grave. He suffered frostbite and caught a chill in his spine. The chill caused inflammation which, in turn, resulted in bone decay. He was admitted to the Grenfell Hospital shortly after, and an operation was performed. The doctor took a bone from Charley's leg and fused it into his back. Charley's days of jumping six-foot fences with both feet together were gone. He no longer shadow boxed around the lumber camps. The operation never completely healed.

One day Charley and another man were crossing Hare Bay, again in a blizzard and on snowshoes. The storm was so severe that they were forced to stop and lay down on the frozen bay. Charley was crazy in pain. His friend examined his back and was shocked to find that the bone the doctor had inserted had

THE PRICE PAID FOR CHARLEY

worked its way out about an inch! Charley asked his friend to use his pliers to extract the bone. After that day Charley remained crippled and grew very sick. The decay in his spine went to his brain, and he died at the age of forty-seven years.

Dr. Baxter T. Gillard of Englee tells the story of Dr. Grenfell's komatik.

"One day just after I became manager of the Englee firm, John Reeves Ltd., the coastal steamer came to our wharf. She had mail and freight for the coast as far away as St. Anthony. It was just after the First World War. Just before she came—a couple of days before Christmas—the northern heavy slob came in White Bay. It was a solid jam. The captain knew that he would not get any farther than Englee, so he put the Roddickton and Conche mail and freight off at Englee. We put it in our warehouse and sent a wireless to Conche, telling the people that their mail was at Englee. Everything was frozen over, and a lot of snow was on the ground.

"The next day four dog teams came from Conche to Englee to get the mail and some of the freight. They stayed overnight at Englee. At noon I left my office and went to the post office. On my way I passed the dog teams that were tied near the fence. While passing I noticed a komatik that looked different than all the others I had ever seen. There was a man tending the dogs, so I asked him who owned the komatik. He told me that it was Vincent Kerry's.

"'What a fine-looking komatik!' I said.

"'Kerry was out sealing that spring when Dr. Grenfell drove off,' he said. 'He saw it near the Grey Islands and picked it up. He has kept it on his store loft ever since.'

"It was Dr. Grenfell's komatik!"

Stanley Hancock, Sr., says that Dr. Grenfell always inquired about people and wanted to be kept informed on the welfare of everyone in his medical zone.

"I remember," said Hancock, "one day I received a wireless from Dr. Grenfell, asking if I'd chair a public meeting for him at the Orange Lodge in Englee. It was on the twelfth day of August. He said that he was coming to Englee in a couple of days. I agreed and wired back to St. Anthony.

"On the sixteenth he arrived and held the meeting. This was a tough time at Englee. There was no food to eat. However, Dr. Grenfell arrived at the meeting and almost every soul in the town was at the hall.

"He gave a stirring speech on the economy. Dr. Grenfell had no use for the fish merchants. He said that we should have an organization! He then organized the Englee Village Council, and I was elected as Secretary of the council. It was the first council of any kind to be organized in our area. And, in fact, I'm the only one living who was elected on that day! What surprised me was that, after he got the council elected, he, being chairman, didn't give us any duties right away. All he said was we would meet at a later date.

"Dr. Grenfell then stood up and thanked all the people for coming. He said in that English tone and in a voice like a trumpet, 'Before we close, we should sing "'God Save the King.'"'

"I jumped to my feet and quickly walked over to him.

"'Dr. Grenfell,' I said, 'before we sing "'God Save the King,'" let's sing "'God Save the People!'"'

"He looked at me and said, 'What do you mean, Stan?'

"'Who,' I asked, 'will sing to the people on the sixteenth day of November, when they are facing a winter of starvation, with not one ounce of food to eat, no clothes to wear, and no medical supplies? The fishery has been a failure. People here don't know where to look, so let's not go singing at this meeting.'

"'Okay, Stan,' he said. 'You come up with a suggestion.' Well, of course the ball was thrown right in my lap!

"'Dr. Grenfell,' I said, 'why don't we elect three men for a committee to go to St. John's and talk with the government about getting something done, like getting a contract of wood to cut?'

"'Okay, Stan, we'll elect you to get the ball rolling.' I had no choice but to accept.

"The meeting closed without singing. I went to John Reeves, the fish merchant at Englee, and told him what we wanted. He agreed to go to St. John's and see the government on the condition that, if he got a contract of pit props—timber used in mines to shore up tunnels—I would be in charge of the contract.

"I agreed and he went. When he came back he had enough supplies for the whole coast, from Harbour Deep to the Fishot Islands. He had a contract of wood and, on the tenth day of December, he had 500 men employed in the woods.

"Ever since that day we've always had food on the table, thanks to Dr. Grenfell."

Stanley Hancock, Sr. worked as a clerk and scaler at a company in Roddickton that owned a large steam sawmill. Aaron Reid worked around the firm as a boat builder in summer and a labourer in winter. The manager of the company, a Mr. Gibbons, was a sick man. One day he called Stanley into his office.

" Stan," he said, "I'm out of medicine and I need more. If not I'm going to be awfully sick by tomorrow."

"What do you want me to do, Mr. Gibbons?" Stanley asked.

"Get a dog team and send to St. Anthony!"

"I don't think I'll be able to get a dog team, sir, because everyone's working in the woods. They're all in the camps."

THE PRICE PAID FOR CHARLEY

"Well, what can we do, Stan? Try and do something for me, will you?"

"Maybe we can send Aaron Reid," Stanley suggested.

"On what?" Mr. Gibbons asked.

"On showshoes!"

"Okay, Stan, okay," he responded in a frustrated tone of voice. "I'll have to suffer it out, I suppose, but tell Aaron to hurry."

"Okay, Mr. Gibbons," Stanley said, and left.

Stanley called in Aaron. "Uncle Aaron," he said, "Mr. Gibbons is in bad shape. His disease is acting up again, and he's got no medicine."

Aaron stared at him. "Well, what do you want me to do, Stan?"

"I want you to go to St. Anthony and get some medicine for him."

"Okay. When do I start?"

"Right away."

Aaron turned to go, but Stanley spoke up. "Get a lunch," he said, "and I'll pack some grub in a bag for you from the store."

Aaron nodded and left the store.

The next day Mr. Gibbons came out of his office into the store, where groceries were sold. Aaron Reid stood before him with a pair of snowshoes under his arm. Mr. Gibbons saw him and rushed over. He was angry and started calling him down.

"I thought they sent you to St. Anthony to get medicine for me!" he complained. "I'm almost dead with pain, Aaron. What am I going to do? I thought that I could depend on you. Why didn't you go?" He turned and put his arms on the counter, and dropped his head onto his arms. He was obviously in pain.

"Mr. Gibbons," said Aaron, "I've got your package right here."

"Who brought it?" inquired Mr. Gibbons, looking up in surprise.

"I did."

Aaron Reid had walked non-stop from Roddickton to St. Anthony, and returned, a total distance of 120 miles, in twenty-seven hours!

The life of Aaron Reid would take many books to relate. One of the Roddickton pioneers, he was known for his boat building in the Roddickton–Englee area.

One day Aaron was especially busy. He worked all day in his boatyard. After supper he cut firewood for the coming winter, then decided to make hay for his cattle. On this calm midsummer evening, Aaron left his boatyard near the Cloud Hills and rowed to the grass meadows five miles away. As young ducks abounded in the region, he took along his shotgun. The game warden was stationed some miles away at Englee, but wildlife patrols were rare, so Aaron didn't worry. He saw broods of young ducks on the water, but he was not interested

THE PRICE PAID FOR CHARLEY

in them. He shot what the old-timers called "non-nesting" birds. They reasoned that any bird unaccompanied by chicks was non-nesting.

As he neared his haystacks, he glimpsed something in the dying sunlight. The sun shone directly in his eyes, and he strained for a better look. Then he saw it: a huge black bear! Bear meat was a treat in those days, and bears that approached towns or cabins were harvested either by gun or snare.

The rising tide made the water deep enough for Aaron to row his boat within ten yards of his haystacks. The bear, seeing him coming, stood up on its hind legs and appeared to challenge him. When the boat touched the shoreline, Aaron picked up his twelve-gauge and quickly loaded it with a slug. The bear started to charge. Aaron, wearing thigh rubbers, stood up in the centre of the boat and took aim. As the animal neared, he fired, striking it in the lower ribs, the hot lead slug lodging in the bear's stomach.

But the bear kept thrashing toward him. Aaron hurried to reload. To his dismay, the empty shell caught in the gun and would not eject. Before he knew it he was being attacked. Throwing down his gun he grabbed his axe. By now the bear was climbing over the gunwale, and it was too close to hit in the head. Swinging frantically, Aaron drove the full blade of the axe into the bear's side.

The animal's momentum struck Aaron fully and pushed him out of the boat. The top edge of his rubbers caught on a thole-pin, leaving him suspended from the edge of the craft with his head and upper body in the water. The enraged bear had full possession of the boat now. It seized Aaron in its powerful jaws and shook him like a rag doll.

Aaron slipped into the water and a red streak rose to the surface. He was in trouble and he knew it. Dragging himself ashore he examined the damage that had been inflicted on his body. The bear had made great gashes on his thighs, and a large muscle on his buttocks was torn, hanging down. Part of his intestines hung out lifelessly. He was losing a lot of blood.

Holding the muscle against his body, he moved his belt down to hold it in place. He took the painter of the boat and wound it around the muscle, reinforcing it and effectively slowing the bleeding. Dragging himself aboard the rowboat, he pushed off. He rowed to his boatyard and called out to his family. Shortly, he was taken to the hospital at St. Anthony, where a doctor performed surgery.

As a result of the ordeal, Aaron became crippled in his legs. It is said that the incident caused his death shortly after in his workshop. The bear was later discovered dead near the haystacks.

Early one summer Monday, William "Billy" Earle left his home at Main Brook, Hare Bay, to fish at St. Lunaire, thirty miles away. He had made the trip many times in his small open motorboat. Uncle Billy, a happy-go-lucky man, told his wife that he would not return home until Saturday evening. He steamed out of the bay with his Acadia engine thumping along through the early morning sunshine. He stopped a couple of times to jig a fish, but caught nothing.

"I'll bet I'd catch this fish quicker than jig it," he said to himself. "When I get to The Oven, I think I'll go in and catch some capelin." Halfway between Goose Cove and St. Anthony lies "The Oven," a large cave at the base of a cliff. The most curious feature of this geological formation is the sandy beach inside it, which is a spawning ground for capelin.

At ten o'clock that morning, Uncle Billy arrived at The Oven. He had no problem getting in. The ocean was not completely smooth, but he navigated the waves with ease and stopped near the beach, shutting down his engine. As he went to the head of the boat to check for capelin, a wave caught the craft and tossed it onto the shore. The boat's keel caught on a rock, and when the sea went out, the boat was left high and dry. It fell on its side and Uncle Billy was thrown out of the craft. Before he had time to look around, another wave came in and engulfed him, throwing him farther up on the beach. Spluttering, he looked around and saw his motorboat smash against the rocks. Five minutes later the boat was full of water, and the undertow pulled it back out.

Uncle Billy could hardly believe what had happened. He knew about The Oven—he had been there many times—but he had never been stranded there!

"Well, well. My boat is gone!" he despaired. The boat was his livelihood. "How do I get out of here?"

He knew that people came to the area every day to get bait for their trawls. It would only be a matter of hours before he would be rescued, he figured.

Evening fell and twilight came, and he knew he would have to wait another day to be rescued. He was painfully aware that, if the sea rose, there would be no escape. There was no place to go and no place to hide. He was at the mercy of the ocean.

The next morning, he shivered near the little sandy beach. Uncle Billy wasn't wearing much clothes, and the cave was cool. He was wet from the spray of the ocean and the condensation dripping from the cliff's solid walls. The sun arose and shone its rays directly into his eyes.

He heard an engine. A motorboat! He was saved! However, several minutes passed and the boat did not enter The Oven.

"What's happening?" Uncle Billy cried. "Why won't someone come in?"

No answer came.

Around noon he surveyed the walls around him. He noticed that, approximately twenty feet up, a shelf stuck out from the face of the cliff's back wall. "Maybe, if the sea heaves, I can get up there," he said. If the place was safe from the heaving sea, a seabird undoubtedly nested there. He realized that it might be his only chance if a storm struck.

Uncle Billy spent all of Tuesday in the cave. That evening he scaled the cliff to the shelf. The outcropping was large enough for him to lay down. He decided against sleeping there, for fear of falling off it while he dreamed.

Wednesday came and went.

THE PRICE PAID FOR CHARLEY

On Thursday the sea hove, and he was forced to climb to the shelf again. The sea was a raging torrent, but luckily it could not sweep him away. It receded during the night, just as Uncle Billy was growing too weak to stand. He was a Christian and he always prayed. "Lord, I only want Your Will to be done, and no more," was all he said in his prayers.

On Friday morning he ate the remains of a dried fish that had been tossed upon the sand. A school of capelin came in. He caught some and ate them raw. He emptied his boots three times a day, and wrung out his socks. Dripping water and condensation had caused the boots and socks to become waterlogged.

Friday night was cool. By now he was extremely weak.

On Saturday morning Uncle Billy sat near the beach as the sun came up. He heard a motorboat, then the sound of the engine cutting its speed. He saw a craft slowly edge its way in. The men aboard were talking to each other, the echo of their voices reaching Uncle Billy's beach over a hundred feet away.

"Hello there!" Uncle Billy called.

The men paid no attention and proceeded to look for capelin.

"Hello! Hello!" Uncle Billy cried as he slowly stood.

One man looked at the other. "Did you say something, George?"

"No."

"I thought I heard something. Shut her off!"

The engine stopped.

"Hello there!" Uncle Billy called again.

"Listen! I heard it again!" said the fisherman.

"Look," said his companion, "there it is! Look! A man . . . or something. Let's get out of here! Start the engine, quick!"

The two fishermen had received quite a scare. They had no idea that what they had seen was a human being!

"It's me! Billy Earle!"

One of them heard the name, then said to his friend, "Just a minute!" He walked to the front of the boat and, in the dull light, saw the man.

"Uncle Billy?"

"Yes! It's me!"

The other man jumped into the water and waded ashore. He carried Uncle Billy back to the boat.

"When did you get here?"

"Monday," Uncle Billy replied casually, as the engine slowly pushed the fishing boat out of The Oven and into the sunlight.

Pictorial Section

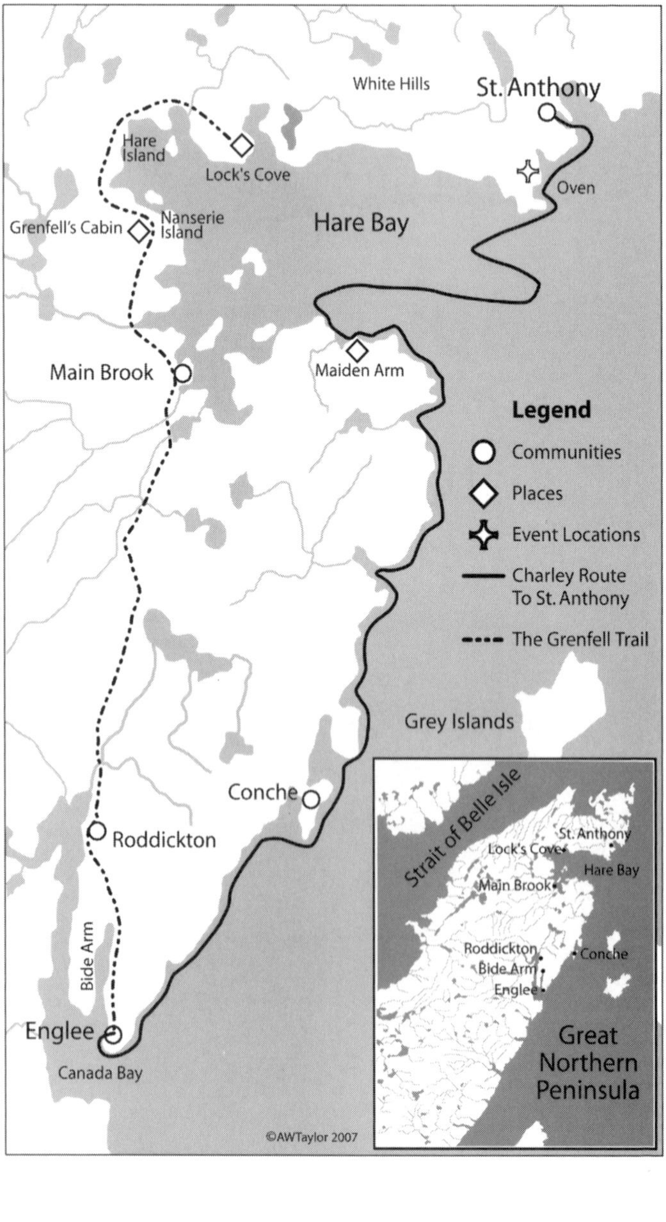
White Hills
St. Anthony
Hare Island
Lock's Cove
Oven
Grenfell's Cabin
Nanserie Island
Hare Bay
Main Brook
Maiden Arm
Legend
Communities
Places
Event Locations
Charley Route To St. Anthony
The Grenfell Trail
Grey Islands
Conche
Roddickton
Bide Arm
Englee
Canada Bay
©AWTaylor 2007
Strait of Belle Isle
St. Anthony
Lock's Cove
Hare Bay
Main Brook
Roddickton
Conche
Bide Arm
Englee
Great Northern Peninsula

THE PRICE PAID FOR CHARLEY

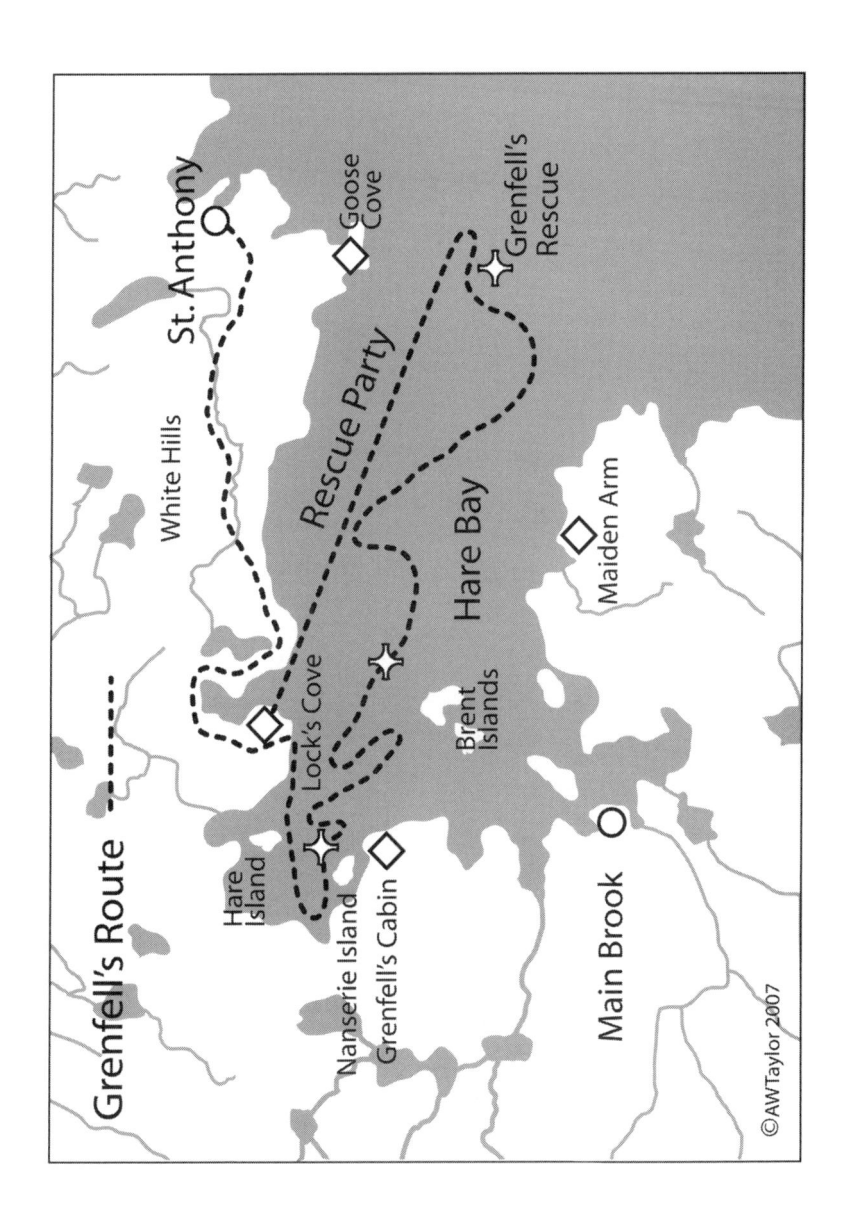

JAMES HANCOCK. THE PHOTOGRAPH WAS TAKEN SHORTLY BEFORE HE DROWNED AT BIDE ARM.

THE PRICE PAID FOR CHARLEY

EMMIE FILLIER, WEARING WHITE ROSES, AT AGE SEVENTEEN. SHE IS SURROUNDED BY JIM HANCOCK'S FAMILY.

THE "SANCTUM SANCTORIUM" AT ST. ANTHONY, GRENFELL'S FIRST CLINIC IN NEWFOUNDLAND.

THE PRICE PAID FOR CHARLEY

Grenfell's first hospital at St. Anthony in 1906.

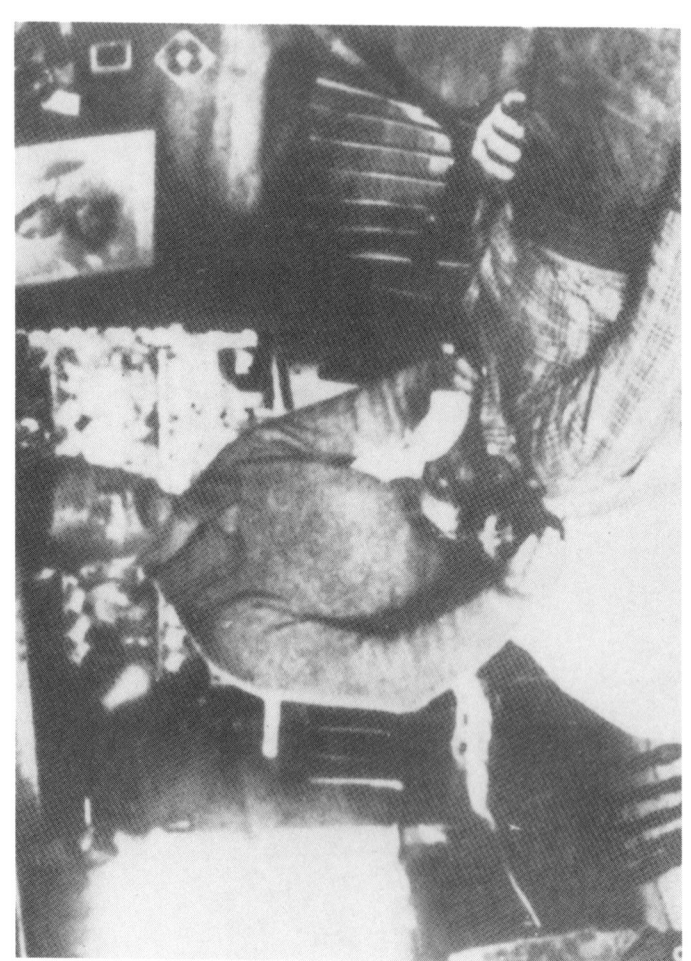

Grenfell giving chloroform to a patient for a rodent ulcer.

THE PRICE PAID FOR CHARLEY

Grenfell's cabin on Nanserie Island.

AARON REID. THIS PHOTOGRAPH WAS TAKEN JUST BEFORE HE WAS ATTACKED BY A BLACK BEAR.

THE PRICE PAID FOR CHARLEY

Levi Dawe and Bill Reid standing in the black punt used to rescue Dr. Grenfell.

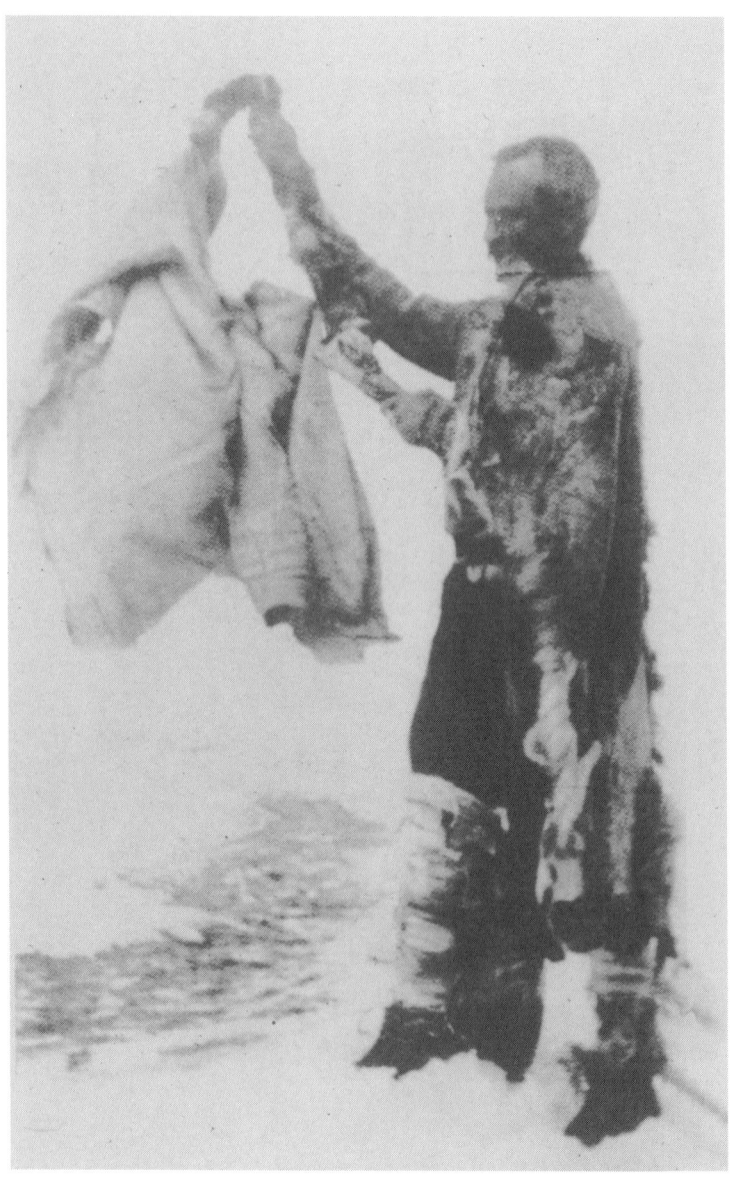

GRENFELL, DRESSED IN GARMENTS HE WORE
WHILE ADRIFT ON THE ICE.

THE PRICE PAID FOR CHARLEY

GRENFELL IN HIS LATER YEARS.
HE HAD A GREAT LOVE FOR DOGS.

About the Author

Earl Baxter Pilgrim was born in St. Anthony, Newfoundland, in 1939. He received his early education in Roddickton, later studying Forestry at the College of Trades and Technology in St. John's. Besides being Newfoundland and Labrador's favourite storyteller and all-time best-selling author, his career has spanned numerous fields. He served with the Princess Patricia's Canadian Light Infantry (PPCLI), during which time he became a champion boxer, and following his stint in the Armed Forces, he went on to become a Forest Ranger and wildlife protection officer with the Newfoundland government. Pilgrim has won several awards for his efforts in conservation and protection of the environment: the Safari International; the Gunther Behr; and the "Achievement Beyond the Call of Duty."

    He is married to the former Beatrice Compton of Englee. They have four children and make their home in Roddickton, Newfoundland. Pilgrim's most recognized literary work is the bestselling Newfoundland epic *Curse of the Red Cross Ring*.